To

MW01235471

E**Q**uip to Lead

The Extraordinary **Power of**
Emotional Intelligence

You are EXTRAORDINARY.

Mike Lejeune & Thecia Jenkins

Mike

ISBN:

First Printing

Editor: Catherine Leek of Green Onion Publishing
Cover Design: Rebecca Councill, CLR Digital Media
Format & Layout: Grace Brown, Pen to Publish

What People Are Saying About
EQuip to Lead

If you want greater influence at work, if you want to be the leader people want to work with and follow, there is no more valuable resource than EQuip to Lead. Filled with real world insights for increasing awareness of your own strengths and blind spots, you are guided with practical, immediately applicable techniques for engaging, coaching or even challenging co-workers. Your future self will thank you for this life changing, career enhancing experience making it possible for you to achieve a level of leadership success better than you have imagined possible.

Rob Pennington, Ph.D., psychologist and award-winning speaker and author of Find the Upside of the Down Times.
Houston, Texas

If you are a leader who wants to enhance your effectiveness and performance but have struggled to do so, then this book is your solution. Mike and Thecia offer practical steps to mastery with loving encouragement and skillful guidance. They take the complexity of EQ and provide a clear path to success, identifying the why, how, and when of applying EQ in your daily life. This is a resource that you will reach for again and again to continue your EQ growth long after you have finished reading the book.

Jill Hickman, SPHR, SHRM-SCP
President, Jill Hickman Companies
Houston, Texas

Any leader who wants to thrive needs to read, study, and apply this book. Emotional intelligence separates the good leaders – and bosses – from the great. Mike and Thecia nail the critical elements for helping your organization achieve your most lofty goals.

Jane Atkinson, Speaker Launcher, Author of Wealthy Speaker 2.0,
Toronto, Canada

EQuip to Lead is a must read for all leaders, aspiring leaders and, for anyone who wishes to develop, nurture and grow their Emotional Intelligence. Engaging and Inspiring! Hone in, as Thecia and Mike share their experiences, that will certainly resonate with many if not all, enabling the reader to self-reflect on key aspects of their own leadership journey, whether it is their leadership style, skills or their relationship building or social skills."

Jacqueline A. Hinds, Certified EQ Coach, Founder Society of Emotional Intelligence International UK & Europe

"Leadership in any form is so critical and I am very happy that Mike and Thecia have provided the techniques to build the needed energy with the required mindset through harnessing the extraordinary power of emotional intelligence skills. It is so timely and significant in this era of Covid-19 with deteriorating energies."

James Kwesi Addison, Certified EQ Coach & Founder Addison International Ghana, West Africa

"The pure magic of this book comes from the combination of the content and the very practical reflection exercises (it's like having a mirror held up in front of your face). With the diverse workforce that we all have to lead in this day and age, Mike and Thecia help us as leaders strengthen relationships by bringing emotion back to the table."

Tanja Faux, Managing Director,
The Talent Experts
Johannesburg, South Africa

"*EQuip to Lead* is an energizing book that will help you lead yourself and lead others to powerfully pursue extraordinary. Mike and Thecia are special people who have strategic insight into you leading you (and others) toward your most amazing future. You're going to love this!"

Jeff Reeter, Entrepreneur, Business Leader, Speaker, Author

"*EQuip to Lead* is both practical and challenging. The way Mike and Thecia describe the power of emotional intelligence is very convincing *and* their techniques will still take some good 'me-time' to thoughtfully consider what changes you will need to make if you wish to be an outstanding leader. My idea: read it in sections – don't just breeze through it on a cross-country flight. Make a few notes on behavior changes that you can commit to. This book will definitely make a difference in your personal and professional lives."

Lou Heckler,
Management Trainer and Keynote Speaker
for more than 40 years

"Mike and Thecia hit just the right cadence in this book – great stories that you immediately relate to, explanations that capture your imagination and the ability to show the price that is paid when we don't increase self-awareness and EQ. This book is very approachable and practical. You and your clients will benefit right away."

Amy Hart, **Trainer/Speaker/Consultant**

EQuip to Lead is a powerful book, packed full of content, and served in a manner of direct application, story telling, and deep author experience. I've read a new books on Leadership and Emotional Intelligence and the challenge has always been the move away from academic foundations and move toward direct life application. Mike and Thecia nailed it for life application. I found the cadence easy to read and came back several times for extra helpings! Anger Management, Fear, and the power of What If threw me out of my comfort zone and into massive leadership reflection and direct application. If you want content, motivation, and specific strategies to implement, this is the book for you.

Curt Tueffert - VP Sales Development, DXP Enterprises,
Houston, Texas

In a hyper-connected world, it isn't a stretch to say we need better awareness of how to manage our thoughts, feelings, and relationships with others more than ever. What immediately grabbed me about

EQuip to Lead is how easy it is to read. It has a personal, intimate style with plenty of anecdotes, and it doesn't attempt to over-analyze or bombard the reader with excessive information. Landmines appear daily in the field of healthy connection to self and others. EQuip to Lead may be our best tool to flourish in this tricky landscape.

Brian Coffman, Vice President hrQ Inc., Sugar Land, Texas

Impactful and thoughtful approach to understanding the importance of our "mindset" as we navigate through our day to day interactions. Provides a different lens to understanding our emotional intelligence and how it impacts our professional and professional relationships. A must for those in leadership roles!

~ Sergeant Donnie Williams, Harris County Sheriff's Office

DEDICATION

To my wife Tommie, my muse whose encouragement and belief in me made these words come alive in my mind and heart. Thank you for being the energy God uses to light my path.

Mike Lejeune

To my community of spiritual and professional mentors who exemplified "emotional intelligence" along my professional journey, thank you for teaching me the value of going above and beyond to create spaces for people to grow.

Thecia Jenkins

ACKNOWLEDGEMENTS

There are many voices who have come together to make *EQuip to Lead* a reality. We wish to thank the following whose voices speak so loudly in the words that you will read.

Our editing team:

Tommie Lejeune, Nikki Lejeune Lopez, and Malini Katzen's attention to detail helped bring clarity to our message.

Our design team:

Grace Brown, Pen to Publish, in laying out the text, and Rebecca Council, CLR Digital Media, for artistically crafting the cover. We were given a gift of Catherine Leek who graciously and creatively edited our words to help us find the true meaning of what we were trying to convey.

A special thank you to every leader who selflessly gave of their time to share their extraordinary thoughts on leadership and emotional intelligence to make this book a gift to all who will read it.

And especially to our Authorized Partners, the Jill Hickman Companies network:

Tamara Atkins, prompting us with her mantra, "Do it Scared."

Amy Hart, lifting us with her consistent affirming words that fueled us.

Jill Hickman, who lovingly kept us on track, encouraging us to take realistic steps that stretched us.

Table of Contents

Emotional Intelligence (EQ) is the ability to manage your thoughts and feelings so that you can more effectively manage relationships by responding and connecting with the emotional needs of others.

Human Versus Business
We Need Both Sides

Do you want more than average from your relationships with others, both at work and home? Thecia and I believe the answer to that is "yes", based on the fact that you are reading about the *extraordinary* power of Emotional Intelligence.

Our Journeys

An exploding market catapulted me into a leadership role at 23 years of age, well before I was ready to take the reins. My first employee was an older guy. Bob was ancient. At 38 years old with an MBA, he was moving to Houston after already having bought and sold a hotel in the Caribbean. And I was supposed to be his boss? We later joked of the strange sound Bob kept hearing in the office. He finally tracked it down. It was my knees knocking together under my desk.

Every day I was flooded with emotions ranging from confusion, uncertainty, massive self-doubt and downright fear. Occasionally, elation bubbled out when we opened a door to a new client, uncovered a purple squirrel of a candidate or made a successful placement. Our relationship grew as I taught Bob our business and he created a safe, supportive atmosphere for me to begin the journey of managing my ego and emotional responses. It was my first journey in seeing the power of Emotional Intelligence in action, how it chiseled the environment for others to engage and grow.

Recently, I read a powerful book, *Do Life Differently.*[1] by Jeff Reeter, a world class leader and financial executive with Northwestern Mutual. I was captured by his subtitle – *A Strategic Path Toward Extraordinary.* The word "extraordinary" raised the bar for what I truly expected for what I wanted out of life – career, financial security, and, what I believe is most important, the relationships I am charged with leading.

Our hearts do not yearn for average, normal or ordinary in our relationships with those who are important to us. Our hearts yearn for extraordinary in the relationships we are blessed with. Friends, family or coworkers in various situations or circumstances create opportunities for us to emotionally engage. What we accomplish or achieve in life is directly tied to our ability to effectively process our emotional interaction with others. A Harvard study[2] reports that success in our careers is determined not by our *IQ* but rather our *EQ*, – our emotional quotient.

I've found that for some, the word "emotion" conjures up weakness, that feelings confound matters. As an authorized partner of the Jill Hickman Companies,[3] our studies have shown there are two sides to every well-run company – the business side and the human side. Our effectiveness as a leader (and top performer) is dependent on being able to successfully navigate both sides. Too much attention to the human side rather than the effectiveness of business systems and processes (and yes profits), and the company will run off the rail.

Today, directing attention towards the human interaction in our organizations is imperative. Gallup polls have recently reported that over 65% of the workforce, both in the United States and globally, are disengaged from their job, their company and more importantly their leader. Our Emotional Intelligence is the catalyst for creating an environment of trust and impacts the communication that makes the vision of the company real and attainable.

And the expansion of virtual work from home environments, either full time or hybrid, can confuse the communication and connection experience for your team. Disassociation is rampant. A recent Monster.com survey showed that 90% of those polled were considering a job change. There has never been a more important need to connect with our teams by establishing an emotionally safe environment.

Getting the Most from These Pages

EQuip to Lead was not written as a quick read. While you can roll through the chapters quickly, you won't gain as much as if you ponder as you read. I'm not sure if you use that word very much, but it means to weigh in the mind, to think about or reflect on.

At the end of each chapter, we've included guideposts to help maximize your take away. Titled "Self-Reflection," they are designed to help you look at Emotional Intelligence through a variety of windows. We encourage you to choose to not skip over the questions. Rather, let them roll around in your mind.

More important than the words we share are the promptings you will receive as you reflect, pointing you toward steps that will not only change your life but allow you to be a catalyst in shaping those who are blessed to walk with you.

We wrestled with what to call these – are they strategies, keys, principles? It became apparent that the mental approach we take, the way we think, has paramount impact on our actions and how we process our emotional responses. We decided on the term "mindsets."

As the words began to appear, while we both share similar mindsets, we had to practice much of what we were writing. True collaboration centers on Self-Awareness, Self-Management and Relationship Management. So, we wrote much in the various chapters in first person, knowing that *I* and *me* could have easily been broadened to *we*.

You can jot notes in the book. Some of you might cringe, like my wife whose mother taught her to never write in a book. We've created a link for you to download all of the resources you'll find at the end of each topic.

http://resources.equip2lead.net

While we've written, edited, and debated the material covered to find our common voice, we've also used personal stories to help you visualize the essence of the message. To help bring additional clarity, to make sure you know which of us is sharing the story, we've included our names in the Table of Contents.

As you ponder the thoughts we are sharing from our experiences and studies our hope and prayer is that you start with the most important tool that impacts your journey to become the amazing being you were created to be – the mirror.

So, ponder away. The journey of self-reflection can be bumpy and at times lonely. We are honored you've chosen to bring us along for the ride. We promise you will be amazed at the insight you will receive and the clarity on steps you can take to impact your life.

We ask that you grab your mirror, and open both your mind and heart. Allow us to guide your steps in the journey to grow as an extraordinary leader, employee, spouse, parent and friend through the *Extraordinary* Power of Emotional Intelligence.

Mike & Thecia

PART ONE

Mindset of
Self-Awareness

There are currently 7.8 billion people occupying space in the world and each have a unique fingerprint.

That means you are unique. You are a masterpiece and, yes, you are a mystery even to yourself sometimes. As an extraordinary leader, self-awareness is the Emotional Intelligence skill that you must develop so you are able to identify your personal strengths as well as areas for growth, and the ability to know your triggers and how to effectively show up in your personal and professional relationships.

Let's start the journey to EQuip you with thoughts on self-awareness.

CHAPTER 1

To Tell the Truth

"You cannot tell the truth about others until you are willing to tell it about yourself."

Virginia Wolf

S elf-awareness is the ability to accurately perceive your own emotions in the moment, and to understand your tendencies across situations. It is understanding what makes you "tick."

Getting to Self-Awareness

How many times have you done or said something that was out of character for you? Do you ever feel unsure of yourself because you feel as if you are living in the body of a stranger?

This is not unusual. Many of us today are so caught up in living and surviving from one day to the next, we seldom take the time to ask ourselves what we like, what motivates or demotivates us, or what we value. These are some of the questions that can lead us to self-awareness.

Self-awareness is key to understanding yourself. According to Kouzes and Posner,[4] authors of *The Leadership Challenge*, it is also one of the indicators of exemplary leadership skills. In order to lead others, you must be able to lead yourself by first taking an inventory of yourself.

I have had the opportunity to provide coaching to executives, managers, and supervisors over the years; and so often I have heard them relate that their greatest obstacle is being self-confident. Self-confidence is built through self-exploration, and that requires a willingness to become vulnerable.

My journey has involved learning to embrace both my strengths and weaknesses and has required a willingness to be transparent. Accepting and including our strengths and weaknesses lays the foundation to grow and to be a part of other's growth.

Being unwilling or unsure about who you are and what you are bringing to the table of relationships (both personally and professionally) creates blind spots that lead to poor communication, low self-confidence, and an overall inability to truly connect.

Understanding when to act, or not to act, is the state of self-management. It is your ability to remain flexible and adaptable while managing your behavior, especially during times of change and resistance.

Owning Your Actions

The average person has approximately sixty thousand thoughts per day; and over half of these thoughts are negative or limiting beliefs.

Most of us spend a great amount of time putting limitations on ourselves and our potential. This is often manifested in thoughts such as:

- "I can't remember names."

- "I could never get a job like that."

- "Some people are just unlucky, like me."

We have all said something along these lines during moments of personal challenge or resistance. It is natural to protect ourselves with these statements, which are based on the emotions of uncertainty, fear, anxiety, etc. The key to learning to "own your actions" is managing your thoughts.

Our ability to self-manage (or to own our actions) can be challenging because we are hardwired to protect ourselves. This function is anchored in our brains in the "amygdala." This small organ, no larger than an almond, is where our memories and emotions associated with these memories are stored. In moments of high stress (positive or negative), this organ is stimulated, and we go into the fight, freeze, or flight zone.

For example, you may be so excited about an upcoming event that you completely forget to take care of your daily, routine tasks. Or, you might find yourself running late. You may even become speechless when, just moments earlier, you had all the right words in your head. Conversely, you may be so fearful, anxious, or intimidated that in the midst of having an argument you either become verbally abusive or simply shut down. This is called an "Amygdala Hi-Jack." You are literally swept up by your emotions.

The ability to manage our actions is essential in our personal and professional development, so that we are able to remain flexible and resilient in the face of adversity, and innovative in our approach to life's challenges.

Your ability to pick up on the emotions of other people and to discern what is going on with them is to effectively communicate and build relationships.

Fostering Relationships

In my opinion, "treat others as you would want to be treated" is an old adage that is incorrect. I believe we should treat people the way they want to be treated.

Personally, I like for people to be direct with me, even if my feelings are initially hurt. The way I see it is at least people are honest with me; I know exactly where they stand. More importantly, their candor allows me to better understand their perception of me. Others may prefer a less direct approach.

Effective relationships are based on "learning" people and what makes them tick. Providing them an opportunity to feel heard allows them to feel validated in their points of view.

Many attendees at my workshops express that they simply want to be heard by their supervisor or coworkers and in their personal relationships. They want to feel as though they matter. It is not always about who is right or wrong, but about acknowledging the other person. When we lean in and listen, we are committing to hearing what is *not* being said. It accentuates the non-verbal cues.

The ability to effectively manage interactions based on your proficiency to identify your emotions and to pick up on the emotions of others builds bonds.

For the first time in our workforce's history, we have four generations working side by side, and our communities are increasingly becoming more ethnically diverse. These evolutions in our workplace and communities, along with many other forms of diversity, can present challenges in managing relationships.

It requires skill and an open mind to understand the perspectives of others while holding onto your own and creating a "win-win" or mutually beneficial situation.

It also requires skill and a willingness to see someone else's potential, and to nurture it, so they can become contributors in the workplace and in our personal relationships. Relationship skills are about fostering trust, valuing differences, and having difficult conversations.

Achieving Emotional Health

Are you emotionally healthy? Emotionally healthy people do things that unhealthy people do not.

Emotionally healthy people do things that unhealthy people do not.

The ability to control impulses and deal with emotional discomfort effectively are two of the most important components of emotional health. Where do you need to stretch, to grow?

However, we can create habits that support these areas. While it's possible to make these changes by yourself, getting professional help can be even more effective. Acquire these traits of the emotionally healthy and you'll find that people will be drawn to follow you as a leader (and build happiness in the home).

Learn more about yourself with these techniques.

- Know your goals.

- Measure what's important.

- Journal your activity each day.

- Try to view yourself as others view you.

- Determine your greatest flaws.

- Ask your friends for insight.

If you know your goals, it's easier to determine how to spend your time in a way that will support those goals. You also learn about yourself by determining what your goals are. If you can't decide on any goals, ask yourself what part of your life needs the most work. Set a goal in that area of your life and stick with it. Your goals don't need to be perfect. Just decide on one that will enhance your life in some way.

Once you know your goals, it's necessary to figure out what's important and then measure those things. If you're trying to lose weight, it would make sense to measure your body weight and caloric intake. You might decide to measure your carbohydrate intake and your exercise, too.

How did you spend your day? Once you know your goals and the relevant activities, measure the quality of your days in a journal. Each hour, write down how you spend that hour. A journal entry might look like: "6:00-7:00 PM: 20 minutes watching TV. 20 minutes exercising. 20 minutes working on my website.

You might be surprised to discover how little time you're actually working toward your goals. Total up the amount of time that you were actually doing something productive. Be honest!

Many of us believe that we're working hard. However, we're often busy doing things that don't affect what matters most to us.

Few of us have an accurate idea of how others view us. This is extremely challenging.

- Ask your friends and family. Beg them to be honest.

- Think about conversations you've had. Imagine someone else said the same things you said. What would you think about them?

- Think about how you handle common situations. Think about how you behave when you're grumpy, tired, stuck in traffic, excited, and so on. Imagine someone else behaving that way. What would you think of them?

Take some time and determine what your greatest flaws are. What are you not good at? In what situations do you struggle? What are your weak points?

Ask your friends for advice and insight. Tell them that you want to become more self-aware. Ask them to describe you, your strengths, and your weaknesses. They will be hesitant to be completely honest. Do your best to convince them that you'll be grateful for their honesty.

Now that we know what emotional health looks like, complete the assessment below to formulate development targets.

Exercise: Emotional Health Assessment

This Emotional Health Assessment brings together activities that emotionally healthy people perform regularly. Use it to determine what key areas you need to target to build Emotional Intelligence. Growth will come from focus while taking steps. Rate yourself on a scale of 1-5 (5 being highest) in the following categories to determine where your strengths and targeted growth areas lie.

1. *Create healthy boundaries.* Successful relationships require healthy boundaries. When boundaries are undefined or unhealthy, the relationship will eventually have a negative impact on your life. Consider where you're vulnerable and create boundaries to protect yourself.

Score: _____

2. *Delay gratification.* Whether you want to finish school, lose 20 pounds, or get your work done before 5:00 pm, it's necessary to delay gratification. For example, eating a cupcake now is more gratifying in the moment than declining. But in the long run, forgoing cupcakes will help you meet your goal of losing weight.

Those who act impulsively and can't delay gratification lack the ability to follow through with wise long-term decisions.

If you make life easy on yourself in the short term, you pay the price in the long term.

Score: _____

3. *Emotionally healthy people can be by themselves.* "By yourself" doesn't mean sitting on the couch with a pizza and Netflix. You're not alone. You actually have two companions with you.

Can you sit quietly, by yourself, with nothing but your thoughts? Or does anxiety about your life create too much discomfort? How much time do you spend distracting yourself from reality?

Score: _____

4. *They are able to adapt to change.* Do you go with the flow or does any change throw you for a loop? Emotionally healthy people are able to roll with the punches and maintain a positive attitude.

Score: _____

5. *Deal with discomfort effectively.* Those who can't deal with emotional discomfort lead chaotic lives. It's only when the discomfort of not taking action becomes so great that they're finally able to do something. By then, it's too late. When you can take a deep breath and take effective action in the face of emotional discomfort, life is a snap.

Score: _____

6. *Love others.* Only emotionally healthy people can truly love others in a positive way. To care, trust, and attach to another person honestly requires good mental health.

Score: _____

7. *Take care of themselves physically.* Do you only eat when you're hungry? Do you make healthy food choices? Are you able to

get yourself to exercise even if you don't feel like it? Do you go to the doctor and dentist regularly? If your emotional health is up to par, you can do these things consistently.

Score: _____

8. *Emotionally healthy people are reliable.* Can people count on you to keep your word? Fulfilling your promises and obligations is one sign of emotional health.

Score: _____

9. *Act proactively.* Are you able to look ahead and see the potential sticking points and then avoid them? Or do you wait until the wheels are coming off before you take action? Living well isn't just about skillfully dealing with challenges. Ideally, it's about intelligently avoiding them when possible.

Score: _____

Self-awareness is available to all, but only pursued by a select few. When you know yourself, it becomes easier to be successful. You can maneuver around your weaknesses. You can take full advantage of your strengths. You learn how to manage yourself and understand what makes you tick.

Self-Reflection

Where do you need to stretch, to grow?

What are your Emotional Intelligence strengths?

In the Exercise above, in which actions did you rate yourself 1-2? What observations do you have of why you chose that rating?

For which behaviors did you rate yourself 4-5? What observations do you have for why you chose that rating?

My three key Emotional Intelligent growth targets and action steps are:

1. _____

2. _____

3. _____

CHAPTER 2

~~∼⌣∽~~

The Power of Humility

"Humility is not thinking less of yourself, it's thinking of yourself less."
C. S. Lewis

I once witnessed the power of humility in the flesh.

A couple of years back, I was blessed with the opportunity to take a few courses on Scripture at the College of Biblical Studies. This was a late-in-life endeavor as I was not someone who grew up reading the Bible, attending Sunday school where favorite verses were memorized. This was a torch lit only a few years ago where I wanted to catch up on something I felt I had missed. Needless to say, as I attended each class, I was overwhelmed by the content.

A Great Teacher's Modesty

One class was led by Dr. Bill Boyd, PhD and past president of the College. He was very educated, consumed with knowledge obtained through years and years of academic research and teaching experiences.

Yet each class period, Dr. Boyd created an environment that resulted in a mixture of pounding headaches, for what we were trying to unravel with our feeble brains, and the rush of enlightenment, as the subtleties of the points he was trying to convey developed meaning and relevance. I sat in the presence of someone who had learned to engage us. To make us want to reach forward requires an atmosphere that is safe to question, safe to ponder, and safe to fail at times.

But the true impact of his teaching came from *the humility* he showed when he revealed the meaning coming from the text we were using as a guide and the lessons buried within the chapters and verses of the Bible. He did not make any effort to impress us with his degrees or experience or knowledge he obtained over the years. Quite the contrary. He used himself as the example of shortsightedness, impatience, and self-centeredness that each of us possesses and most go to extremes to try to hide. These examples became a mirror for each of us in his class to look at our own lives, our own journeys to find true meaning and application for our studies.

I found myself wanting to make a point of how I saw the connection of each clause we studied to another; to impress him with my so-called newly revealed insight that I was sure had some semblance of divine guidance. And I was not alone in the class experiencing this impulse (fortunately). The patience he exuded as he focused on each of us to try to understand our point of view, no matter how far-fetched, was easily read in the twinkle of his eyes and smile. Instead of pointing out our frail thoughts as meaningless, he gave merit to how we might have come to that conclusion, never putting down our concepts or efforts.

Finding My Humbleness

It struck me as I drove home that as men, as leaders, as fathers, as husbands how often do we try to exert power and authority at work and home instead of compassion and emotional safety? How often do we attempt to feel significant by giving direction coupled with how-to mixed with must-do, and does all that come across as ego driven instead of caretaker?

As a man I struggle with how I am perceived in my house and in the office. I want to be understood, I want my guidance to be followed, my decisions adhered to. That night I saw an example of the influence someone could have by focusing outward rather than inward, by seeking out needs instead of satisfying an ego, by using our life mistakes as a canvas to teach instead of war stories from the old days where we thought we slew some form of dragon.

Humility allows you to focus on the task in front of you.

There truly is power in humility. Humility allows you to focus on the task in front of you. Avoid allowing puffed up pride to cloud your senses and throw you off your game.

This is what our families and the people we are responsible for need from us.

Self-Reflection

Humility is the key to being respected and appreciated. Even though I am proud of my accomplishments, am I careful to tone down my external excitement?

In what types of situations am I comfortable with openly expressing my excitement?

Are there times I'm offended by someone else's victories? How do I respond when I realize someone is offended by my victory?

CHAPTER 3

~⌒~

The Emotional Drain of Perfection Versus Excellence

"Excellence is not a skill. It is an attitude."
Ralph Marston

T here's a huge difference between doing something well and doing it perfectly. Attempting to be perfect can bring on feelings of inadequacy and even interfere with completing important projects. Excellence, on the other hand, is attainable and is always more than good enough.

Eliminate the idea of perfection from your life and you'll see your productivity soar. For example, a poorly written, but complete book can still be published. On the other hand, a perfectly composed book that's only half finished is essentially worthless. Of course, there's a middle ground between poor and perfect. And that terrain includes excellence.

Eliminate the idea of perfection from your life and you'll see your productivity soar.

The problem with perfection is that it can never be truly attained. So, in pursuing perfection, not only are you doomed to fail, but, in the end, you also might have nothing to show for your efforts.

The Law of Diminishing Returns

Apply the Law of Diminishing Returns when striving for perfection.

Imagine if you spent 25 hours on a two-page paper for a college class. Would you get an A? I would certainly hope so, but what else may have suffered because of it? What about your other classes and obligations? Maybe instead you could have done something enjoyable.

The other thing to consider is this: could you have gotten an A with two hours of work? Or five? From a practical standpoint, the same results can often be attained with much less time and effort. There is nothing to be gained by spending more time on something than truly needed.

If you spent six hours washing and waxing your car and your neighbor spent two hours on his, do you think anyone could tell the difference a week later? More importantly, what else could you have accomplished with those extra four hours? Life is short, and there's a lot to do. What else could you do with your time besides trying to be perfect?

Pursue Excellence Instead

Of course, you'll want to decide on the level of excellence you wish to attain before getting started on a project. Everything you do should have standards that you strive to attain. If you choose your benchmark of completion properly, there's never a good reason to go beyond that point.

What exactly is excellent, anyway? In our discussion, excellent means that the task was completed at a level high enough that there's no cause for concern. That is, you know your work will meet whatever requirements are put upon it And, regardless of the nature of the task, you know that it's done well enough and you have zero concerns about it.

When deciding how well a project really needs to be performed, consider the possible outcomes if the task is completed at various levels of quality. Obviously, a surgical instrument requires a much higher level of quality than a spoon.

Once the proper level has been set, you now have a target – a goal that's been chosen with some thought and intelligence. Now, simply execute the task to that level and stop. That task is completed, and it's time to do something else.

Giving up a habit of pursuing perfection might seem challenging. However, you'll be happier, more productive, and you'll maintain your sanity much more easily by striving for excellence instead. Focus on exceeding expectations. In terms of time, quality, and productivity, excellence always wins in the end.

Exercise: Twelve Signs that You're Being Too Self-Critical

It's admirable to do your best and attempt to be the finest person you can be. It only makes sense to examine your negative results in life and try to do better the next time. But it's also easy to become too self-critical. A high level of self-criticism is detrimental to success and good mental health. Excessive self-criticism hurts your self-esteem and confidence.

Consider these signs that you might be too critical of yourself.

1. *You're paralyzed.* One sign that you're overly critical toward yourself is a lack of action. If you've been stuck in the same situation for an extended period of time, you're too hard on yourself. Otherwise, you'd be out there taking care of business and making positive changes to your life.

2. *You're slow to forgive others.* When you can't forgive yourself, you're unable to forgive others. When you can let go and forgive yourself, you can do the same for the other people in your life.

3. *You're never pleased with your accomplishments.* It doesn't matter to you that you shaved 10 minutes off your best 10K time or graduated from medical school. You're bothered by the fact that you didn't win the race or attend Harvard medical school.

4. *You're not assertive.* You have to be comfortable with yourself to feel comfortable with asserting yourself. Assertiveness also brings the risk of rejection. Being too self-critical can increase the fear of rejection from others.

5. *You consistently say bad things to yourself.* There's little harm in a small amount of negative self-talk. But a constant barrage of self-criticism is highly damaging. Imagine telling your child

that they can't do anything right and should give up trying. It sounds crazy when viewed from that perspective.

6. *You're a chronic underachiever.* Underachieving is both a symptom and a cause of self-criticism. Consistent underachieving is a call to action!

7. *Others feel comfortable being critical of you.* The average person isn't comfortable criticizing others. However, after they've heard you criticize yourself repeatedly, they're likely to feel they can join in on the criticism.

8. *You criticize yourself in general terms, rather than just for specific events.* There's a difference between telling yourself that you're not a good tennis player and telling yourself that you're not good at anything. General criticism is false and highly damaging. A lack of success at a particular activity doesn't make you flawed at everything. It's illogical.

9. *You keep your opinions to yourself.* While you have every reason to avoid telling your neighbor she looks fat in her dress, you should feel comfortable sharing the title of your favorite book. If you don't feel comfortable sharing your opinions freely, you're too concerned about being judged by others or saying the wrong thing.

10. *You spend too much time dwelling on your mistakes.* Can you move on quickly after a short period of self-reflection or do you dwell on your mistakes for an extended period of time?

11. *You find yourself unable to ask for help.* It shouldn't be difficult to ask for help. In fact, the more help the better! Are you afraid

of being viewed as incapable? If so, you're too critical of yourself.

12. *You can't give yourself a single compliment.* Everyone is good at something. Or maybe you know you're good at a few things but don't think you deserve a compliment. Either way, you're being too hard on yourself.

You're sabotaging yourself by being overly self-critical. You limit both your success and your mood. Realize how much you harm yourself with self-criticism. Learn from your mistakes and apply the information with enthusiasm.

Self-Reflection

Does everything have to be perfect or else you deem it a complete failure?

Thinking back to the exercise in this chapter, might you be too self-critical?

What does the difference between perfect and good enough mean to you?

CHAPTER 4

~~~

Embracing Feedback ... Perception Is Reality

"Other times, you're doing some piece of work and suddenly you get feedback that tells you that you have touched something that is very alive in the cosmos."

Leonard Nimoy

I sn't it interesting where (and when) you will get an opportunity to learn? For me, it was while having my blood drawn for my annual physical.

Feedback to Action to Perception

When learning I was a professional speaker on the subject of leadership and raising the productivity of our best performers, Rita asked if I heard of James Hunter's servant leadership principle.[5] She proceeded to dig through her cabinets, then handed me the CD series she had just listened to. I asked her what caught her attention regarding the subject of leadership, as Rita was not in charge of the office. Her role was to serve as a phlebotomist (always loved that term), serving clients by drawing blood samples.

Rita explained that while she always got rave reviews from her clients, her coworkers were not as enthusiastic about her in-office demeanor. They found her somewhat aloof and defensive. Her next statement was one that should speak to anyone, but especially those of us who are both challenged and honored with the opportunity to serve in a leadership capacity.

"At first I was taken aback by what I thought was the fallacy in the way I was viewed. Then I decided if I wanted it to change, I was the only one who could make it happen."

After getting feedback from her coworkers, Rita focused daily on three simple action steps that would change the way she was perceived by the team.

1. *Stop nit-picking.* In every office there are things that get overlooked or not done to acceptable standards. Rita decided instead of whining or being confrontational, she should keep her mouth shut, and step up to take responsibility for what she witnessed. She became part of the solution, helping to raise standards by serving as a better teammate.

2. *Change facial expressions when listening.* Many times, while we are absorbing information, our face stiffens. If someone is saying something we don't agree with, our face may show more intensity than what we are feeling. This creates a belief that we are unapproachable, insensitive, or uncaring. We need to listen with more than our ears. Our eyes and facial expressions are great conduits for improved communication.

3. *Soften the intensity of your voice.* While our passion can be a great asset to the team, the volume in our voice can be

counterproductive. Our intensity can serve to shut down how receptive people are to our message and create an image that we are pontificating from a soap box rather than simply expressing our feelings on the subject. Loud volume can send a message that we are self-absorbed rather than empathic to those around us.

Rita has received feedback from teammates that they see a marked difference in her.

What is fascinating is Rita's heart is the same it has always been – focused on the needs of those she serves and works with. What has changed is her effectiveness in demonstrating her tremendous heart. Feedback changed her actions which changed how others perceived her.

How have you tried to change perception in your professional life?

Giving and Receiving Feedback

Ask yourself, "Do I agree with the following statements?" If no, why not?

I love feedback.

Feedback is a precious gift. I love receiving feedback and sharing my observations with others.

Listening to others teaches me how my behavior affects those around me. I benefit by considering events from a different perspective than my own. Others may see things that I overlook.

I invite feedback by being friendly and open-minded.

I express my enthusiasm and gratitude. I ask questions and take notes to show that I am interested in what my friends and colleagues have to say. I rephrase the input I am given to ensure that our understanding is accurate.

I look for practical ways to apply the information, and I change my behavior and track my progress.

When I want to give feedback to others, I choose an appropriate time and place. I act promptly so issues can be dealt with in a timely manner. I speak directly and tactfully while still being respectful and caring. I consider the needs of others instead of focusing on what I want them to do.

I acknowledge that constructive feedback can come from many sources. A stranger may point out something useful.

Feedback can be positive as well as critical. I enjoy the praise and recognition I receive. I take time to compliment others on their talents and accomplishments.

Today, I welcome feedback. I appreciate the opportunity to learn from others and share my perspective. The knowledge I gain helps me to grow wiser and stronger.

Self-Reflection
What is the difference between feedback and advice? Why do I sometimes feel threatened by feedback? When? What are my strengths when it comes to giving feedback?

CHAPTER 5

~⌒~

Can't Nobody Do You Like You Do

"Be who you are and say what you feel, because those who mind don't matter and those who matter don't mind."

Dr. Seuss

I was hired to speak at a conference for a group that I had spoken for the year before, so I was excited to return. On the day of the conference, I arrived in time to hear the person speaking before me. I like to arrive early and get the vibe of the room. I also take notes to connect to the previous speaker during my session.

Being Authentic

Not only was the speaker great, but her presentation covered just about everything I had planned to speak about. I sat there mortified, thinking "I have to follow her and basically give the same address." Finally I got up halfway through her talk and quickly walked back to my room. My heart was racing, my head was throbbing, and that darn inner critic was having a field day in my head. After having an amygdala hi-jack, I decided to take my own advice and simply take three deep breaths and calm down.

I often say it is okay to talk to yourself as long as you say something smart back, so I began to speak to myself using positive self-talk. The speaker before was amazing and I had to make the decision that even though our presentations were similar, the reality is I had my own unique way of sharing my content.

After pulling myself together, I went back to the conference room. When I was introduced, I strutted up to the platform and did *my* thing, *my* way. I used my time to engage and provide interactive activities, including a hotseat session to help the attendees implement and act on the information they had the privilege of hearing, not once but twice.

The result? Attendees came up and shared how much they enjoyed and loved the opportunity to engage with the activities. Yes, they saw the similarities but they were served by the individual way that myself and the preceding presenter had shared similar information.

Leadership and owning a room mean recognizing that you are not the only one that has access to information. The differentiator, however, is your delivery of the information. Your emphasis should be on being authentic and sharing from your perspective. That is the beauty of diversity and why it is a necessity in leadership. You can share one message with a team of one thousand and each person will share their learning in a way that is unique to them. The lesson I learned that day is never compete or feel inadequate because someone has the same message as you.

The Dangers of Comparing Yourself to Others

Comparing yourself to others is a reliable way to reduce your confidence, motivation, and self-esteem. It must be natural to make these types of comparisons, because nearly everyone does it. However, that doesn't mean it's a good move.

If you want to become the best possible you, avoid comparing yourself to others.

The Dangers of Comparison

There are several challenges that occur when you compare yourself to someone else. For instance, everyone has a different starting point. You might be just learning to play golf, but your friend has been playing for ten years. You might be interested in playing basketball, but you're only five feet tall and your friend is eighteen inches taller than you are. You can't compare progress, results, or success unless the starting points are the same, and they never are.

> *You can't compare progress, results, or success unless the starting points are the same, and they never are.*

Some people are born with a high IQ. Some people naturally have amazing hand-eye coordination. Others have a natural knack for music or math. Everyone has a different level of talent. Again, different starting points.

The resources available to you and another person will be different. If you want to play the violin and your father is a wealthy concert violinist, you have a huge advantage over someone born into a financially-challenged family that has no experience in music.

You don't compare your Texas Hold'em skills to your neighbor the electrician. You compare yourself to the tournament winners. We don't compare ourselves to the average. We compare ourselves to the best the world has to offer.

There's always someone better. There are only a handful of people that can make a reasonable claim to being the best at anything. There are nearly eight billion people in the world. That's a lot of people you have to surpass to be the best.

It's easy to see why making comparisons can be dangerous. There's little to gain and too much risk. Comparing yourself to others doesn't provide useful information. You're only going to upset yourself, and that type of comparison isn't fair in the first place.

Some Solutions

To avoid the dangers of comparing yourself to others, here are some remedies you can try instead.

- *Compare yourself to yourself.* A better option is to compare yourself to yourself. Pay attention to your progress over time. Notice your improvement. As long as you're making headway, you have a good reason to be excited! Strive to become better each day.

- *Limit your exposure to social media.* In theory, social media exists to connect people. In actuality, social media is often used as a way of showing off.

  o You rarely get the real story. What you get is someone's best attempt to make their life look better than it really is. Everyone, except you, seems to be living a spectacular life. It's not true.

o Be cautious with social media. Most people report being happier when they remove social media from their lives.

- *Use the success of others as inspiration.* The success of others can be useful to you. You can study how they became so successful. Their success can inspire you to become the best you can be. Just avoid comparing your success to theirs.

Do you compare yourself to others? Making this type of comparison can be detrimental to your confidence and self-esteem. Instead, compare your current version of yourself to the version of yourself from three months ago. That's a fair comparison to make. It becomes easy to see your progress or lack of progress.

The best comparison you can make is to your past self. Set a few goals and spend some time each day working on those goals. You'll be happy when you see the progress you've made.

Self-Reflection

What are my attributes that would make someone want to or enjoy working with me?

How often does comparing myself to someone else cause me to feel inadequate? Who am I comparing myself to? What are the circumstances?

What story in my past highlights the impact I have had on someone's growth, development, or well-being?

PART TWO

Mindset of
Self-Management

Have you ever experienced being on the edge?

You want to respond to a question and yet cannot seem to pry your lips apart to speak your peace. In a flash you find yourself unable to keep words from pouring out of your mouth and regret them as soon as they hit the air. You are faced with a decision and ruminate for weeks, months, and, yes, sometimes even years. Then later you regret that you did not "just do it." You easily find yourself waiting for others to make a move, or you make decisions impulsively.

This is what lack of self-management looks like in our daily lives. The Emotional Intelligence skill of self-management is the ability to manage our mindset and our actions or reactions. How well are you managing your beliefs, attitude, feelings, and ultimately your behavior?

It's okay.

Move to the next level of becoming an extraordinary leader and explore the art of action and accountability.

CHAPTER 6

~~~

Who's in the Driver's Seat?

"Between stimulus and response there is a space. In that space is our power to choose our response. In our response lies our growth and our freedom."

Viktor Frankl

We all struggle with the decision to "go to neutral" when emotions well up, such as anger, hurt, frustration, rejection, disappointment. I remember working on our farm, driving tractors and at times getting the equipment in a bind. Dad taught me the importance of finding neutral, to allow the machinery to relax and remove the tension allowing it to unbind. Then, slowly determine how to move it forward or reverse, whatever the situation called for.

Failing to Go to Neutral

Go to neutral is something I wish Scottie Pippin had done in Game 3 of the 1994 NBA Eastern conference playoff. Scottie has often been hailed as one of the greatest athletes to play for the Chicago Bulls, possibly in all of professional basketball. Yet with 1.8 seconds to go and the game tied, the Bulls' coach, Phil Jackson, called time out to design the last play. Rather than calling for the ball to go to Scottie, he chose Toni Kukoc. Pippin's response was startling. "I'm not leaving the bench if I don't get the shot."

Scottie's anger, hurt, and rejection of not being the go-to guy, like Michael Jordan (who had retired at the beginning of the year) had so often been called, kept him off the floor. Ego and emotion overshadowed and used up a career's worth of good will.

The story ends with Kukoc hitting the shot, and Scottie leading the team to victory in two more games before being eliminated in Game 7.

Well, unfortunately the story didn't end there. It's now thirty years later and today Scottie's answer to an interview question is still filled with emotion, calling Jackson a racist for going with Kukoc rather than him. He is still not in neutral, and his response shows the focus remains on ego rather than the team victory. A factor that could have weighed into his response was it was finally Scottie's team, not Michael's. It was his turn for the glory of the last shot. But what could have factored into the coach's mind is that in the fourth quarter Scottie had only made one out of five attempts at scoring.

In the heat of battle, failure to go to neutral became a decision that is now career defining for him.

When accepting the role of leadership, our responsibility to those who choose to follow us is to keep the focus on the higher mission, many times requiring our egos to be put in our pockets. We must go to neutral, let the tension subside, allow the situation to unbind, and then find the proper gear to accomplish what you and the team are driving toward.

Overcoming Frustration and Disappointment

Are there times when you've been working hard to make progress on something or to just get it completed, yet despite your best efforts, it isn't going well, and you feel frustrated and disappointed about that?

It can feel like you're running through mud, using up all your energy, but you're not getting very far at all!

Experiencing these kinds of disappointments can be really stressful, especially if you are up against a time constraint. You can very easily become totally despondent, and then despair creeps in. The good news is, however, that you can get past this. You will get past it, as others have done before you.

The project that you've been working on likely isn't the issue. Maybe you were in line for a promotion. You thought you would get it but didn't. Maybe you are trying to explore the possibilities of a completely new career, but after all the effort expended, you still have no idea what kind of new career might be best for you.

This is simply a part of life, and nearly everyone has been in this place before. Some of us have been there many times. When we get in these situations, it's important to find different ways to move us over, under, around, or through them and not spend too much time dwelling on them.

To overcome your frustration and disappointment, you only need to spend enough time thinking about your circumstances to get a good handle on the situation. Then, take action and create a change in the way you are seeing it.

The fastest and most effective way of altering anything is to make a decision and take action. Consider some of the actions below which others have used to make a positive difference.

Try reframing the situation. It takes on a whole new perspective. View the frustration that you are experiencing as a good thing because frustration means that you are just about to learn something. Look for the lesson, and once you've found it, you will never need to go back there again.

Change up your routine. Your daily schedule has a bigger impact on the way you show up in life than you think. If you find yourself in a mindset that is not supporting you, change your routine.

Go for a run, ride your bike, or go for a walk. Go somewhere different, go in the rain. Get close to nature. Do something exhilarating. Your whole demeanor will change for the better in sixty minutes or less and so will the challenge that you are wrestling with.

You can seek encouragement and inspiration from others. Who do you know who can inspire you? Encourage you? Share some life wisdom with you? We all have someone we respect, trust, and enjoy talking over difficult situations with. Oftentimes, just explaining the situation can shine a light on a solution or a strategy that can resolve a difficult issue.

Try adjusting your attitude. It's not what happens to you; it's what you do about it that matters. Acknowledge that you are in a place of frustration and disappointment, but also acknowledge that you can and will get past it. Other people have, and so will you. There is nothing that is insurmountable. Start from the viewpoint that there is a solution, and you will find it.

Acknowledge that you are in a place of frustration and disappointment, but also acknowledge that you can and will get past it.

Getting good at anything is easiest done by learning from other people's experiences. Always be open to new ideas, different ways of seeing things, additional strategies, and especially new attitudes.

More often than not, it's not the situation or circumstance that is the root of the issue. It's either the way we are approaching it or the way we are perceiving it. If someone else has a methodology for resolving these issues, don't reinvent the wheel, but follow in their footsteps.

If you adopt a perspective of positive expectancy, whereby you know that it doesn't matter what happens, and you're absolutely certain that everything will work out perfectly, more often than not, it really does.

If you can get this one habit into your daily affirmations, everything will change for the better.

Don't let frustration and disappointment rule over you. Use these methods and tips to get past them and move forward toward the future you want!

Exercise: The Seven Day Challenge

For the next week, review each day and consider your answers to the questions below.

- How did you spend your time?

- What did you enjoy?

- What did you dislike?

- Did you lose your temper or experience depression? If so, why?

- What was the best thing that happened to you? What was so great about it?

- What was the worst thing that happened?

- What would you change about the day?

- What did you learn about yourself today?

- How did you do in your relationships today? What did you learn about your teammate? What could you have done better?

Action Steps

After answering each question above, run through the action steps that follow and determine if you've been applying them.

- Practice self-discipline: What are three things that you know you should do but have been putting off? Do them and congratulate yourself for your self-discipline!

- Think of a decision that you've been struggling to make. Look at the situation from a long-term perspective. Ask yourself, "Is this the way? What are your best options?" Pick one and run with it.

- Describe an instance in which you had trouble controlling your emotions and demonstrated poor emotional self-regulation. What were the results?

- Describe an instance in which you were able to control your emotions and demonstrated strong emotional self-regulation. What were the results?

- Make a plan for how you can respond positively and effectively when your negative emotions are triggered.

Self-Reflection

For me, the emotion that is hardest to take out of gear and put into neutral is _____

Questions I need to ask myself (besides "have I taken a breath") are

_____

_____

_____

_____

What can I do to help others on my team lower intensity and find neutral?

_____

_____

_____

_____

CHAPTER 7

～～～

Managing Anger

"The greatest remedy for anger is delay."
Thomas Paine

The start of my junior year in high school was a watershed moment for me. While I should have been a starter on our basketball team, six games into the season I found myself riding the bench along with Mark, one of the seniors.

Competitive Anger

In a game with the LaGrange Gators, one of the largest schools in the state, our small school found ourselves drastically behind. At half time, to ratchet up our performance, Coach CJ Scheufens gave an in-your-face address. Mark exploded, demanding "I'm going to be put in the game in the second half or else I was quit." Without taking a breath, Coach walked to him and told him to sit down. "I quit! I'm tired of this!" Mark exclaimed and walked out. Without words, Coach glared at me across the locker implying, "So, what are you going to do?"

We all face turning points and decisions in our lives where anger wells up. It is an emotion that comes from being human. The question is how do we process it?

The third quarter started with me in the spot I had been growing accustomed to, on the end of the bench. With three minutes left to go, Coach called time out and asked a simple question, "Are you ready to play?" I leaped forward, ripped off my warm-up jacket and stared straight into his eyes.

"Yes, Sir!"

You need to know I didn't say it out of respect. It was anger! All the rage and frustration came boiling out as I hit the court. As the opposing team inbounded the ball, I began to cover my opponent with a full court press, stealing the ball and driving toward our basket for a lay-up. Next, one of my teammates stole the dribble from the player he was guarding and lobbed the ball to me in the corner of the court, where I sunk a 20-foot jump shot. With venom coming from what seemed like every pore in my body, my opponent had no chance. I sprinted back to play defense on our end of the court, again deflecting a pass and led a breakaway for another lay-up.

I strode toward our bench when the LaGrange Coach called time out to regroup. CJ stood in front of me with a glare similar to what I had just witnessed at halftime, this time with words, he said "Where have you been? Now, that is basketball!"

Helpful and Unhelpful Anger

Anger is an emotion that comes along with the human spirit. It can be offensive to those who experience it being delivered in an uncontrolled manner. Anger becomes dangerous when it becomes the tool of the tongue, when words attack a person and not the problem being faced. It also becomes useful when it fuels steps that need to be taken, sparking inaction to catapult into action. Anger can launch us past roadblocks, obstacles, and barriers. It ignites the heart. Uncontained anger, however, blocks the mind.

Emotions that are pushed down, especially anger, will have a tendency to build pressure that will find a way to be released.

Emotions that are pushed down, especially anger, will have a tendency to build pressure that will find a way to be released. Does it become a powder keg, exploding when we don't communicate our anger in a productive manner?

We didn't win the game against LaGrange. The score remained lopsided. What did come from that night was the beginning of me seeing how to harness the energy emotions create and direct it toward desired results. I saw my teammates' performance rise as my emotion, released in an appropriate manner (although my opponent might disagree of its appropriateness), created energy and synergy.

Exercise: Anger Worksheet

If anger is an emotional response that needs to be shifted into neutral, consider the four stages of anger listed below. Under each stage, write the physical signs and thoughts that you experience during that stage.

The four stages are:

1. The buildup – annoyed and irritated

2. The spark – a trigger ignites the fuse

3. The explosion – the emotional outburst

4. The aftermath – the calm after the storm

Emotional intelligence affects your relationship in so many ways! Use this worksheet to build your Self-Management skills. Your teammates at work and home will be pleasantly surprised by the difference.

Self-Reflection
Consider ways you can be aware of the early signs of anger to prevent the explosion. How can you deal proactively with annoyances so they don't morph into full blown angry outbursts?

CHAPTER 8

～～～

It's Soft Skills that Drive the Bottom Line

"You cannot continuously improve interdependent systems and processes until you progressively perfect interdependent, interpersonal relationships."

Stephen Covey

Elaine is a professional who holds an MBA from one of the top business schools in the country, speaks two languages, and is meticulous in her work. However, today she was passed over for a promotion for the third time in the last eighteen months. As she drives home, she clenches her steering wheel and unleashes a trail of obscenities through tears as she tries to make sense of why her supervisor would say, "Your inability to work effectively with peers continues to be an issue."

Developing Your Emotional Intelligence

Technical competencies play an integral role in climbing the proverbial corporate ladder or expanding your business. However, according to Daniel Goleman, a Harvard psychologist, it is our ability to manage our emotions that will ultimately determine our success in the workplace and deliver on the financial bottom line. Emotional

Intelligence, the ability to manage our emotions and identify the emotions of others, is a soft skill that empowers you to address the hard issues in the workplace.

Like Elaine, many individuals have stellar technical skills while their ability to recognize their anxiety level, express their thoughts in a non-confrontational manner, identify the strengths of team members, or experience empathy in the workplace are non-existent. These may seem unimportant, but the reality is that many a deal has been lost in corporate America because an individual was not made to feel important or felt that their needs were not being met by the representative of the company negotiating with them.

Have you ever been in a meeting and suddenly found yourself frowning, tapping your fingers, or making a comment and then wishing you had rephrased your words? Chances are someone or something triggered an emotion in you. Self-awareness is key in moving forward in both personal and professional relationships. Take time to know what pushes your emotional triggers before you are front and center in a business meeting or professional setting. Practice on your response, ask yourself if the triggered emotion is real or are you reacting to internal fears.

Let's review some strategies to win in the business zone by developing your Emotional Intelligence.

When irrational thoughts or fears taunt you regarding your abilities or the comments and actions of others take over your thoughts, talk back to yourself. Tell yourself that you are skilled and also be willing to process the comments of others to see if there is any validity in their observations. Take in that information and then coach yourself to use it to enhance your performance. Remind yourself that you are good at what you do and that you are willing to learn from every interaction you have in the course of your day. Also tell yourself that there is no failure, only feedback.

Take some time on a daily or weekly basis to visit with staff or departments within your company, to see people at work in their element. Become a tourist in your company: Ask yourself – and them – what is important about their work, what are their daily triumphs and struggles, what excites them about their role. Being effective with people means learning about what motivates and demotivates them and what develops trust. Take time to know your team and what is important to them and allow them to know what is important to you.

When you know yourself and know your triggers, you are able to rationalize your irrational thoughts and have established relationships with your team. The next step is a willingness to engage in crucial conversations versus letting issues go unresolved in the workplace. Set a time to meet with your colleague or subordinate, and agree to disagree. Next, allow the other person to give their point of view without interruption, and then give your point of view. After that, attempt to find common ground and agree to work collaboratively on the outcome together as a team. The most important parts of the conversation are learning to hear each other out and to respect each other's diverse points of view and, ultimately, what is best for the bottom line of the business.

Start today to work on your soft skills and address the hard issues in the workplace that will result in bottom-line results and put you in the zone for expanded business.

Clear the Air

Difficult conversations are, well, difficult. We don't like to have them with others. We don't like others to have them with us. Consequently, we aren't very good at them because we avoid having them as much as possible.

A lot of challenges can be avoided by sitting down and having a difficult conversation.

However, many situations only get worse without having a conversation. A lot of challenges can be avoided by sitting down and having a difficult conversation. Take a deep breath and do it. Try these tips to clear the air with a simple conversation.

- *Consider the other person's point of view.* Before going to war with someone, take the time to see things from their perspective. They might have a valid issue that you haven't considered. It's not easy to do this, but those who deal with people effectively are good at seeing the other's viewpoint. Think about what the other person knows and wants. Sometimes others don't have all the information that you do.

- *Identify the issue.* What exactly is the problem? You might think your employee runs for the parking lot each night because they don't care. The real situation might be that they have to pick their children up from daycare by a certain time or pay a big fine. Be certain you know what the actual issue is before having a difficult conversation.

- *Identify the desired outcome.* What is the goal of the conversation? Is it to end a relationship? Find middle ground?

It's hard to achieve success if you don't even know what success looks like. Determine what you're trying to accomplish before you have the conversation.

- *Right place, right time.* Most difficult conversations need to be done in private, and at a time when everyone involved has enough time to participate and process their thoughts.

- *Identify behavior but leave the person alone.* Suppose you don't like the fact that your husband leaves his wet bath towel on the hardwood floor of the master bedroom. An appropriate tactic is to say, "Leaving your wet towel on the floor is causing damage and creating a tripping hazard. I would appreciate it if you would hang up your wet towel." It is less effective to say, "Why are you such a lazy person? What's wrong with you?" This approach might feel good in the moment, but it always backfires. When you attack others, their natural instinct is to attack back. That's probably not your desired outcome.

- *Allow the other person to speak.* Conversations require at least two people. You can't just drop a bomb and then head for your poker game. It's important that everyone has a chance to say what's on their mind.

- *Forgive.* Difficult conversations often result in hurt feelings. Forgiveness is part of the process of finding a pleasant place to land. Holding a grudge only creates additional pain. Forgiving another person can be incredibly challenging, but you'll feel a lot better.

- *Do something positive afterwards.* Avoid just going back to your neutral corners afterwards. It creates an awkward situation. Go for a walk or go to a movie. Have some ice cream. Something to take the edge off.

Whom do you need to speak to? What would be solved by having that conversation? Difficult conversations are called difficult for a reason. They're not easy conversations to have. They make both parties feel uncomfortable.

However, the ability to communicate clearly and precisely is one of the advantages of being human. We have an obligation to use that ability. You can do it.

Feelings of Defensiveness

Have you ever gone into defensive mode after someone criticized you? Your walls go up and all you want to do is shift the focus away from the critical remark.

Defensiveness describes ways in which we react towards another person after they pass judgment on us. It's a coping mechanism that happens after being disparaged. As opposed to listening to the censure, when someone is defensive, they shift focus away from the criticism by criticizing back or giving someone the silent treatment.

Instead of dealing with the conflict or criticism, defensiveness shows up as a way to protect yourself.

Everyone has felt defensive before. It's a completely normal reaction to criticism. However, in the long run, defensiveness can block us from both connecting to others and growing as a person.

There are a few reasons why people may react to criticism with defensiveness. Maybe they did not receive the unconditional support that makes us feel confident as children. Defensiveness could also be a result of anxiety or poor assertiveness. Sometimes, defensiveness also reflects guilt or shame that a person wants to keep hidden.

Overall, defensiveness stems from fear or insecurity.

Overall, defensiveness stems from fear or insecurity. If someone is defensive, that defensiveness gives them an illusion of control. However, if we are constantly defensive, deflecting criticism or blame, how can we grow or become closer to others?

Are you wondering how defensiveness might play out in your relationships? There are three common types of defensiveness that we might display when we react to criticism.

1. *Ad hominem attacks.* These are attacks on someone's personal character or history, directed against a person rather than the position they are maintaining.

2. *Silent treatment.* The silent treatment is when silence is used to punish someone and make them feel hurt.

3. *Bringing up the past.* This looks like bringing up something someone did in the past to use against them instead of dealing with the criticism or issue at hand.

Remember, defensiveness is a completely normal reaction, but it can prevent you from getting closer to those you love. To strengthen your relationships, you can implement different strategies to feel less defensive.

Practice noticing your defensiveness. The first step to overcoming your defensiveness is being able to notice how it shows up in your daily life. Work to identify what events trigger your defensiveness.

When you notice yourself becoming defensive, be transparent about what you are going through. Identify the feeling. What feelings does defensiveness bring up for you? Are you defensive because you feel sad? Angry?

What do you need at that moment? Letting the person know that you feel guarded and communicating what you need is a great way to invite them in to help you feel supported. Some examples of needs might be acceptance, safety, support, touch, communication, consideration, compassion, empathy, or to be understood.

Think about the intention behind a comment. Sometimes, we hear criticism from someone else and immediately perceive it as an attack. But what is the person saying? Take a moment to reflect. Are there different ways you can interpret what they said?

Breathe. When you feel yourself becoming defensive, calm your nervous system by taking three deep breaths. This may sound simple, but our brain needs 20% of the body's oxygen to think with clarity. Clarity reduces defensiveness and it will help you to quiet yourself and allow you to focus on resolving the disagreement.

Most importantly, accept responsibility for the role you play in each situation. Learning to be accountable can help you get closer to your partner and grow as an individual.

Remember that disagreements are a natural part of any relationship – work, romantic, or otherwise. It's normal for someone to constructively bring up something that can be improved.

When you find yourself getting defensive, take a few moments to think about the intention of what is being said. Can you see the good in the intentions? Is there any area for which you can take responsibility?

Self-Reflection

Are there nonverbal cues you might be giving that send the wrong message to someone you are connecting with?

Is there someone you need to have a crucial conversation with to clear the air and refocus the relationship?

What negative message is broadcasting in your head that you need to turn down or get rid of?

Who do you need to spend intentional time with to learn more about what is important to them?

CHAPTER 9

~~~

Do You Create or Drain Energy?

"Few men during their lifetime come anywhere near exhausting the resources dwelling within them. There are deep wells of strength that are never used."

Richard E. Byrd

PowerPoint slide I made for a virtual presentation keeps running around in my head. It centered on how to answer the question, "What is the new norm?"

Average and normal will not create enough energy to turn the tides. As the business marketplace experiences interruptions, normal processes that create energy slows. I once hired someone from a national recruiting machine to join our company, which I referred to as a premium boutique company. After four months I watched in confusion as his productivity sputtered, never firing to the levels he claimed to have previously accomplished. Eventually I realized that what was missing was the monolith he had previously worked for churned energy through a massive influx of data, the people who sought the company out, and the overflow of opportunity from working with a large cross-functional team. When he joined us, he had to create his own juice every day, all day.

Each of us must fight the droning questions, "Is catastrophe around the corner (probably not), will the job market return, will unemployment fall (always has, always will)?" Psychologists are pointing to studies on how draining our current situation is. To lead with Emotional Intelligence, the atmosphere of uncertainty requires leaders and followers alike to be energy-making machines.

To lead with Emotional Intelligence, the atmosphere of uncertainty requires leaders and followers alike to be energy-making machines.

Micro Blocks

Do you create energy or drain it?

Energy is generated from shifting broad beams of light with the pinpoint accuracy of lasers. The same is true in managing our time. We don't have eight-hour days. We have a day broken into eight one-hour blocks. In rethinking the calendar into blocks of time, we start creating energy.

We create power when we manage ourselves with "micro blocks." Challenge yourself to focus your attention on the most pressing activity you have for forty-five minutes, which is much less than doing something for an hour. How much territory can you cover in forty-five minutes? How many business development or recruiting outreaches can you initiate in less than an hour? What administrative mound can you whittle? What steps can you take on a project you are charged with?

Thecia and I used this technique to write the book you are reading. Fear of failure, not completing something we are both passionate about is a recurring battle we faced as we launched into creating a roadmap to guide you on increasing your Emotional Intelligence. After spiraling for a few brainstorming sessions, Thecia threw down the challenge to see how much we could move in an hour if we kept our focus on a single item that would move the ball.

This is more than a mind game. It's keeping your attention on the most important objective you have and pushing with intensity to make it a reality (like writing this book). Then after forty-five minutes, take fifteen minutes to reset and replenish. Spend time with the kids, talk to your spouse, walk up the street to stare at the trees. Walk down the hall and wave at someone if you've gone back to the office (social distancing rules apply). Then return to your desk to sprint toward another micro block and the next set of objectives. The micro block is designed to create energy that comes from focus.

Someone's ability to create their own energy has a high influence on their Emotional Intelligence scale. We can honestly say it is an attribute that has never been needed more, both at work and at home. Small snippets yield high returns. Micro blocks make the engine hum and puts a muffler on the negative voices that drain energy.

Unable to Just Sit Down and Do Your Work?

Have you ever had important things to do, but you just couldn't make yourself do them? Sometimes it's simple procrastination, but that's not the only explanation that applies when you're resisting your work. There can be many reasons keeping you from getting your work done.

Are your goals inspiring you? If you can't get yourself to write for your blog, start your online business, or begin on a big project at home, perhaps your objectives aren't the right goals for you. When you have inspiring goals, motivation is much easier to generate. Do you know the why behind your ambitions?

It's hard to get busy when you only have a vague idea of what you need to do. Be crystal clear on your intention and what you want to accomplish. We all know we have things to do, but are you certain of what exactly needs to be done?

Our brains don't like confusion or ambiguity. We reject uncertainty, so clarify your task until you're certain of what you need to do, and *why*. Understanding the importance, the impact of what you are trying to achieve is the fuel that creates energy.

Fear of failure is one of the greatest and most common obstacles to getting work done. If you look ahead and see failure in your future, it's very challenging to sit down and get busy. Consider, instead, what will happen if you succeed! Focus on *this* outcome.

Perhaps your ability to focus is weak. We have too many distractions in our lives these days. Our lives are overly complicated. Our ability to focus has atrophied. Practice focusing for short periods of time and your ability to focus will improve quite quickly. Set a timer for short burst of activities. A friend gave me a thirty-minute hour glass that drains the sand in half of an hour. I use it to increase focus.

And get rid of as many of the distractions in your life as possible. What is a distraction? Anything you find yourself doing instead of what you should be doing. The most important question you can ask yourself? "Is what I'm doing tension relieving or goal achieving?"

How many balls are you juggling? Maybe you have too much going on in your life, and you simply lack the physical and emotional energy to do your work. Minimize your life, uncomplicate things. Keep the essential steps toward the most important goals that you want to see come to reality.

There is always a price to pay for our action or inaction. It is the price of discipline or the price of regret. There may not enough pain associated with *not* doing something. An important question to ask is, "What will I (or someone else) experience if I don't take that step, do that task?"

Clear focus is the key ingredient for getting your work done and making real progress.

Self-Reflection
When do my best ideas come to me? How much time do I spend engaging in those activities? What are five challenges in my life that I would like to solve? How could I make use of my creativity to come up with possible solutions? What could I do to enhance my creativity?

CHAPTER 10

~~~

Understanding and Managing Your Emotional Triggers

"The amygdala in the emotional center sees and hears everything that occurs to us instantaneously and is the trigger point for the fight or flight response."

Daniel Goleman

Maybe you wonder what's really going on when you feel like certain events push your buttons and knock you off course. Take control of your emotional triggers by increasing your awareness and developing new ways of responding.

Becoming Aware of Your Emotional Triggers

A trigger is an experience that draws us back into the past and causes old feelings and behaviors to arise. An ice cream sandwich may remind you of summer vacations or gossiping coworkers could bring back images of high school cliques.

Some triggers are situational and social – external prompts. Many people tend to eat more at holiday gatherings. If your spouse is tense, it may affect your own mood.

Other triggers come from internal causes. Over time, anything can be internalized. Even when you're surrounded by loved ones, you may be carrying around old conflicts that interfere with your ability to live in the present moment.

Much of the literature about triggers focuses on addictions. It's important to remember that memory plays a powerful role in all our lives and realize that we all have triggers.

If you're startled by loud noises that your spouse fails to notice, you've seen how differently people react to the same stimulus. Accepting individual differences and taking such variety into account improves communications and relationships.

Disciplining Your Emotional Triggers

Identifying and understanding your emotion triggers is one task, but learning to manage them is quite another. However, there are some techniques and practice will make it easier.

Tracking your triggers is often the first step in mastering them. It might be helpful to keep a log of occasions when you experience intense emotions or engage in behavior you want to change. Note what's going on in your head and in your surroundings at the time.

The key to change is placing yourself in difficult positions and being open to doing something new and more constructive.

Challenge yourself. The key to change is placing yourself in difficult positions and being open to doing something new and more constructive. If worrying about money is keeping you up at night, call your creditors to arrange payment plans.

Proceed at your own pace. Start out by being more assertive with your spouse and friends if you need to practice before talking with your boss.

Take advantage of quiet times to brainstorm new strategies and alternatives you can use when you are under pressure. List productive and enjoyable activities you can substitute for gambling or other habits you want to break.

Reducing daily stress will make it easier to handle intense emotions, so make time to relax. Begin a daily meditation practice or start out the day by listening to instrumental music during your drive to the office.

One simple way to make yourself more resilient is to take good care of your body and mind. Eat right, sleep well, and exercise regularly. You'll be better prepared to bounce back from any obstacles that may arise.

Close family and friends are vital to feeling validated and nurtured. Develop a strong support network. When you're dealing with stubborn issues, it's good to know you have people who care about you and want to help.

The more you know about your own triggers, the more insight and compassion you can develop into what the people around you may be struggling with. Strive to be a little more patient and forgiving and people will be more likely to do the same for you.

If you're having trouble making progress on your own, professional help could make a big difference. Ask your physician or people you trust for references or call the psychology department at your local universities.

We all have our own unique emotional triggers. Learning to handle them constructively enables us to fix the issues that get in our way and move ahead in life.

Your Emotions

How can you manage your feelings if you don't know what they are? Only about one-third of adults can accurately identify their emotions, according to the bestselling book *Emotional Intelligence 2.0.*[6]

Maybe you were discouraged from expressing your feelings when you were growing up. Maybe you judge yourself harshly for becoming angry with your children or jealous of your partner.

Whatever the reason, *bottling things up could be holding you back.* Discover a new and more constructive approach to getting in touch with your emotions.

In order to identify your emotions, you'll need to employ a few strategies. Try the ones listed below.

- *Name your symptoms.* Try to label what you're feeling. Make your language as specific as possible. Sadness could mean grieving for a lost pet or feeling listless on a rainy day.

- *Look deeper.* Keep in mind that your behavior may be deceptive if you tend to cover up feelings that you think are inappropriate. For example, do you hesitate to show affection because others might take advantage of you? Examine your true motives.

- *Listen to your body.* Physical sensations can reveal important clues about your emotional state. A clenched jaw and furrowed brows could indicate anger. Relaxed muscles and a warm glow suggest you're happy about something.

- *Pray or meditate regularly.* Create a quiet time and place for exploring your emotions. Observe your feelings without making judgments.

Then you'll be ready to see the benefits of connecting with your emotions. From gaining personal insight to increasing your productivity, there are many advantages to accepting and acknowledging your feelings.

Connecting with your emotions helps you gain self-knowledge. Increasing your self-awareness enables you to develop and grow. You can clarify your goals and direct your energies toward the activities that are meaningful to you. It's the first step in living with a sense of purpose instead of operating on autopilot.

Understanding yourself and others also makes greater intimacy possible and enhances your relationships. You'll be more sensitive to how your loved ones are likely to react to any situation, and you'll be able to provide more empathy and moral support.

Any challenge is easier to overcome when you're able to identify and regulate your emotions. You'll have the motivation and skills to deal with setbacks without letting them undermine your self-esteem. You'll build resiliency.

Emotional awareness also maximizes your productivity. Linking with your emotions will help you achieve more. You can collaborate effectively with others and make sound decisions under pressure.

Finally it is time to share your emotions. You've done the hardest work, now express what is behind your behavior and actions.

Practice putting your emotions into words. Tell others how you feel and why. Allowing yourself to be vulnerable can be scary, but the rewards are worth it. You'll connect on a deeper level and feel more secure.

Start small. If certain subjects seem too sensitive, you can prepare yourself by discussing things that feel less risky. As you become more confident in your skills, you'll be able to address larger issues with ease.

In addition to conversation, physical activity can be another outlet for strong feelings. After a rough day at the office, invite your coworkers to join you for a CrossFit class or a long walk. Tensions may melt away without saying a word.

Art projects can tell the world how you're feeling too. If you struggle with painting or sculpting, you can choose any medium that works for you. Just do something creative. Pour your heart into baking cookies or designing a board game.

If you need more help dealing with your emotions, ask your physician or friends for recommendations for a counselor you can talk with. Therapy can be a safe place to process past experiences and try out new behaviors.

> *You may feel uncomfortable temporarily as the emotions you've ignored come to the surface but stick with it.*

You may feel uncomfortable temporarily as the emotions you've ignored come to the surface but stick with it. Increasing your emotional awareness will prepare you to be a more effective leader and strengthen relationships at work and home.

Self-Reflection

What actions will I implement to:

- Connect with my emotions;
- Identify my emotions; and
- Share my emotions.

CHAPTER 11

~~~~~

How Do We Deal with Turmoil?

"WHAT and IF are as non-threatening as words can be. But put them side-by-side and they have the power to haunt you for the rest of your life."

Lisa Friedman

Today's news cycles offer minimal clarity, only a future of chaotic uncertainty. Cascading stock markets. Plummeting oil prices. Political attacks from all quarters creating an atmosphere of descension. And near pandemonium caused by the spread of the COVID-19 virus. (I wish someone had the foresight to advise me to take a long position in the stock market on toilet paper.)

So, what are our options as we battle this climate of fear?

Focus

So much of the angst we are experiencing centers on what might be instead of what is. Not that what you wish for or are afraid of won't come to pass. With the price of crude oil falling off the cliff and some energy stock prices cut in half, I was anxious to speak to Tiffany Wallace, president of Dagen.

Since her firm is a leader in finding talent for the energy market, I wanted to know how she has navigated the growth of her company through turbulent waters. She replied, "Every day, connect with people who are going to be important to you in the future."

Are you focused on building what you want or are you tightening up with the fear of what you won't have?

Take Steps Every Day

Actually, you should take steps every hour: I find myself fighting the battle of "what if," creating painful images of what the future *could* hold. It's caused by trying to control my situation or circumstance and protect me from potential pain. We are wired to be pain avoidant. Watch a child touch a hot stove one time, see what their hand does the next time it gets close to the stove.

I tripped in my front yard while chasing my dog in an attempt to keep her from being run over by an oncoming car. The misstep caused a fall that broke both of my arms. Due to a diagnosis of a non-union fracture in one of my arms, the healing process was not optimistic. The image of a crooked arm, not capable of lifting any weight was tormenting. One doctor recommended surgery, another said to trust the body and begin small steps of rehab for the left arm and right shoulder.

I chose the second. In rehab, I learned that consistent steps, even when sometimes in pain, strengthens muscles and heals bones. Yep, one of my wise counselors, Dr. Mark Hendry at Frostwood Chiropractic explained that putting pressure on my arm would actually strengthen the bone.

Today's fear-filled marketplace can freeze us into not connecting. COVID-19 is not the only virus. The Internet is filled with examples of how fear is contagious. Look at hoarding and runs on food supplies at the grocers.

Pursue Action

Rather than stockpile information, choose to act. It is important to be well informed. Today, however, the number of microphones droning on eats away time and attention under the falseness of productivity. The Internet is flooded with reprocessed information that appears to be an avalanche waiting to happen. I'm not minimizing the healthcare issues or the economic constriction in the marketplace. Obtaining the "latest news" to find out how bad things really are, in many circumstances, is a time waster.

Alejo Orvañanos, a dear friend and an international, high net-worth financial advisor for Bank of America Merrill Lynch pointed out that information doesn't make you rich or poor, only the action you take.

Or as we discussed, sometimes it's the action that you *don't* take. I remember seeing an opossum on the power line behind my house, frozen with fear as Benson and Katy, my two large dogs, barked as if a dinosaur had invaded their sanctuary. Sitting on the line motionless did nothing to calm the dogs. The varmint experienced safety only when it went into action, pursuing its goal of reaching the next pole.

Create Momentum

I'm not a great skier, so my confidence was somewhat limited when I strapped two pieces of wood on my feet and felt like I was throwing myself off a mountain. I had to force myself to gather speed by turning down the mountain, creating energy to allow me to make the turns. When I was at a standstill, trying to turn my skis resulted in me falling over like a domino. As soon as I had the courage to look down the mountain, not at where I was, energy was created that actually brought control over my direction. Looking at where I was headed was a learned skill. Fear made me want to look down at the ground beneath my skis, to agonize by overthinking.

As I looked down the mountain toward the village and my destination, what I learned from my ski instructor was to look where I wanted to go and the skis (and my body) will follow. Take steps to build momentum.

I reached out to Ben Meador, the founder of the Meador Companies, one of the leading staffing firms in Houston, which just celebrated its 50th anniversary. I had witnessed how Ben had to face the challenge of shepherding his company through markets where the floor fell out suddenly and painfully. His message is one that we all need to embrace. "You just have to keep everything in perspective because the sun will be beaming through the clouds in time so we all just have to keep the faith."

Every day, seek the sun that is always on the other side of the storm.

That's not just false optimism. It's truth. Every day, seek the sun that is always on the other side of the storm.

Self-Reflection

The vision I see for my future is _____

_____

Is there something I hesitate doing that could lead me to my goals and dreams?

What steps do I need to do more consistently?

_____

_____

_____

_____

CHAPTER 12

~~~

The Power of *What If*

"Most of the things about which we make decisions, and into which therefore we inquire, present us with alternative possibilities."

Aristotle

What if has had both a paralyzing and catapulting effect on my life.

At the age of 23, I began the battle of severe panic attacks. The first attacked happened on an elevator, then an airplane. Their existence extended to driving across bridges, movie theaters, and spread to standing in lines at grocery stores. I found myself removing the possibilities or *what ifs* by withdrawing from any event where they might raise their head.

What if was a question that began to freeze me into non-action. It became my worst enemy. Through counseling, medication, and prayer, the dread has been lifted. Today *what if* has become my best friend. Here is the change.

Change the Direction of the Question

The question is no longer:

- *What if* something you are afraid of happens?

- *What if* something you want doesn't happen?

- *What if* someone might get upset by what you say (or even might say)?

- *What if* ... fill in the blank?

Of the things we worry about, 99% never happen. So, *what if* we change the direction of the question.

The first *what if* is based on circumstances that I might (usually might not) face. It is a thought I can't control. However, the second *what if* is a call to action that I can control. Its power propels us forward into action, starting mentally then physically. It begins the process of moving us into motion, the place where all success starts.

So *what if* you created a list of things you haven't done that you feel guilty about – a call not placed, a note not sent, a doctor's appointment not scheduled. Something you feel you dropped the ball on by not following up. What if you acted on those today, replacing the guilt with action?

So, *what if* you reached out to three people to connect with who might seem intimating. In sales, it might be a prospect higher up the food chain than what seems comfortable. Maybe it's someone you have long wanted to meet. Replace intimidation with action.

So, *what if* a project you've started seems stalled (or worst put on a shelf for "later")? Even though you don't have an answer, what is a step you can take to keep the ball rolling until the answer presents itself (in one way or another it always does). One of the principles the Navy

Seals use to battle adversity during a mission is the power that comes from focusing on competing targeted small steps. Each breeds confidence as the mission moves forward. The only option is focusing on steps toward completing the mission.

You may not be dealing with high levels of anxiety, yet is something freezing you in place, tethering you to perceived limitations? Try asking yourself the question *"What if* I did ..." to find three steps that can move you forward. By the way, those three steps lead to the place dreams are made.

Motivation to Do Things You Don't Want to Do

It's likely that your biggest challenge isn't that you don't know what to do. It's that you can't reliably get yourself to do what you know you should do.

If you could get yourself to do the hard things, you could successfully follow any diet, any exercise routine, stay away from your ex, keep your house clean, save money, or ask for that promotion. You'd never procrastinate.

We're all severely limited by the things we can't get ourselves to do. We know plenty, but we have poor self-management skills. It's hard to think of a skill that could impact your life more. But, there are ways to change your life by getting more control over yourself.

Consider what you have to gain by taking the undesirable action. What are the rewards of getting this task done? What do you have to gain? Make a long list of benefits and use logic to your advantage.

Consider what you have to lose if you don't complete the task. Now, do the opposite. Imagine the worst that can happen if you fail to act. Make a list of everything that could go wrong. What are the disadvantages of putting this task off? Make it painful to procrastinate.

Next, focus on how great you'll feel when it's finished. Visualize completing the task. Concentrate on how wonderful it feels. Imagine all the benefits you'll gain. Notice how happy you feel to finally have this monkey off your back. Now do the opposite. Vividly visualize not doing the task and experience all of the negative consequences. Make yourself feel as horrible as you can. Don't worry, it's in your best interest!

Imagine doing the tasks and notice where you feel tension in your body. Keep thinking about performing the task and relax those uncomfortable areas of your body. When you can think about the task and not experience a negative reaction, it will be much easier to perform that task.

Sometimes, the best way to get yourself to start is to start small. It might be a single phone call, five minutes of work, or cleaning out one closet. Break your task down into bite-sized portions that you can handle with relative ease.

Break your task down into bite-sized portions that you can handle with relative ease.

And promise yourself a reward. That's right, bribe yourself. Perhaps it's a candy bar, dinner with a friend, or a new TV. Avoid being silly and putting yourself into debt. But desperate times call for desperate measures.

Here is an easy way to motivate yourself to do something. Give a friend an amount of money that's really meaningful to you. It might be $10 or $1,000. Now, tell your friend not to give it back to you until you've completed the task. You can really turn up the heat on yourself by giving yourself a deadline. Tell your friend they can spend the money if you don't complete the task on time!

Get the action, goal or result you are seeking out of your head and on paper or computer. The act of putting it in writing reduces the mental spin and helps with clarity. Then make sure you look at it.

If you could get yourself to do everything you knew you should do, your life would be unrecognizable. You already know enough to have a much, much better life! Information is hardly the problem these days. However, we still aren't any better at managing ourselves.

If you can master this one skill, everything is within your grasp. All you really need to do is learn how to get yourself to do the hard things. If you can do that, life is easy!

Ten Ways to Push Beyond Fear

Fear is the biggest roadblock to success. Fear is a constant companion if you're attempting to grow and achieve. The most successful people are often those who manage fear most effectively. Those who manage fear poorly are often the least successful. Learning to push beyond fear is a valuable skill that greatly increases your odds of success.

Conquer your fear and achieve success with these practices.

1. *Control your thoughts.* It's possible to think about anything you choose. The best way to stress yourself is to think about stressful things. You're not more effective when you're afraid; you're less. That doesn't mean you should bury your head in the sand, but put yourself in a frame of mind that makes you most able to deal with the situation.

2. *Consider the worst.* Take a moment to consider the worst likely outcome. Can you handle it? Can you maneuver in a way that makes the worst outcome manageable? If you know you can handle the worst, there's no reason to be afraid. Be prepared for the worst and you'll find it rarely occurs.

3. *Breathe.* Focus on your breath and slow your mind. Your mind will take reality and run wild with it. Focusing on your breath will calm your mind, and reality remains. When stress is at your doorstep, just stop and breathe.

4. *Imagine a positive outcome.* Raise the level of your expectations. Your fear will melt away if you expect something positive to happen. Create a future that you find exciting and visualize your fear away. Repeat this exercise several times a day. Eventually, you'll begin to believe it.

5. *Exercise.* Physical exertion is an excellent way to burn away your fear. It's hard to feel afraid when you're exhausted! Go for a quick run, a long walk, or lift weights. When you're pleasantly out of breath, you'll find your fear has lessened.

6. *Get support.* Talk to friend or a mentor. Be choosy! Some of your friends and family are more supportive than others. Find

someone going through the same thing and console each other. Online forums can be helpful, and you can remain anonymous.

7. *Understand that change and fear go hand in hand.* There's a reason to be excited when you're afraid; it's very possible that you're at the beginning of a great change in your life. Nothing seems to change when you're comfortable 100% of the time. Be excited that you're doing something that creates feelings of fear. Your life may be about to change for the better.

8. *Make a list of the benefits of moving forward.* Create a long list of the positive results that could result from being brave. Give yourself several reasons to motivate yourself. For example, if you're starting a new business, your list might include the following: create a greater income; do something you love; finally realize your dream of being an entrepreneur. Not to mention you'll have the amazing experience of overcoming your fear!

9. *Do it anyway.* Fear is a lousy reason for not doing something. It's not a good excuse, though it is a socially acceptable one. Be brave and resolve to do the thing you fear. It will be easier the next time. Build your tolerance to fear by facing fear daily.

10. *Celebrate small steps.* We have a tendency to give credence to big strides, landmark accomplishments. By focusing on what you've achieved rather than what you haven't, you gain the fuel necessary to continue the journey. Fear is battled with a series of steps that turn into giant leaps.

Do you allow fear to determine your actions? Fear is a self-imposed roadblock on the path to progress. Developing the skill to handle fear appropriately is necessary to move forward in any aspect of life. When you feel fear, you're on the verge of making a significant change in your life. Get excited!

Self-Reflection
The *what if* of fear I need to remove from my thoughts is_____   _____   The *what if* of hope I need to add to my thoughts is_____   _____

CHAPTER 13

Leaders Control the Weather!

*"Ten percent of conflicts are due to difference in opinion. Ninety percent
are due to wrong tone of voice."*

Unknown

I t's been fun researching best practices of world-class leaders. When
I interviewed Scott Eblin, president of the Eblin Group for the
Leadership Strategies for Tomorrow's Leaders, I was stunned
when he challenged me with this statement: *Leaders control the weather!*

After letting it sink in, he continued that in the office the leader
literally throws a switch on the atmosphere the team members function
in. Is it stormy or sunshine? Peaceful or gale force winds? Do we ask
our people to perform their best with the weather we create?

In the third edition of *The Next Level*, Scott outlines drivers that
help leaders do a better job of controlling the weather as they climb to
new roles and responsibilities. You would think that a key factor was
learning to better handle the new situations and objectives. What he
points to is the importance of determining what you need to let-go of
in order to move forward. Since next level situations require different,

new results, there is an emphasis required on letting-go-of skills, behaviors, and mindsets, all of which may have helped in the past role.

Your ability to climb the ladder, open new business units or take on a startup requires intellect. Effective leaders are pretty good at learning new things but the letting go is much more challenging. Picking up is a cognitive challenge. Letting go is more of an emotional challenge.

> *Picking up is a cognitive challenge. Letting go is more of an emotional challenge.*

I love the performance formula for growth: $P = p - i$. Performance equals your potential, minus the interference. There is external tactical pressure that attempts to drive us off course. Yet the biggest interference we sometimes face as we stretch is the emotional baggage of managing ourselves first, in order to better leverage our team and engage our colleagues.

The greatest emotional battle we face in stepping toward new horizons is fear. What if we fail? What if we don't achieve what is expected of us? What do we expect of ourselves? To fight the fear of the unknown, we sometimes throw blankets over what we don't know to protect others from seeing areas where we might feel inept. Letting go of control and accountability without releasing responsibility is key for growth to take place.

Imposter Syndrome

I smiled when Scott spoke of the battleground of the Imposter Syndrome. When asking how many people in the audiences he speaks to have felt "Oh my gosh, if they only knew what I don't know, they would have never chosen me for this role," or "How in the heck did I even get here in the first place?" he said the rooms are filled with hands in the air. As we discussed this, my mind flashed to when I was asked to serve as president of the National Speakers Association in Houston.

I had only finished two years on the board and was early in building my speaking business. It seemed that when I looked around the room at every meeting, I saw a sea of people with so much talent and capabilities that seemed greater than mine. I had a choice to make. Do I bluff my way or ask for input and help? Fortunately for me (and the organization), I chose the latter. I watched as people became more engaged, took on more responsibility and ownership. The atmosphere became electric. Not because of me, but rather because of us.

Letting Go

I had to shift to what Scott pointed out was "letting go," making a shift from being the go-to person to the leader who builds and nurtures teams of go-to people. I've seen the past president of our NSA Chapter, Amy Castro, become a master at this. The association is raising the bar on programming, educational outreach, membership growth. The more she let go, the more people stepped up. It is a prerequisite for growth when the scope of the role of the leader becomes too big.

If you're going to scale your leadership, you cannot be personally responsible for everything. You're accountable for it, you absolutely own the results and the impact of the results, but you don't do it all. That's how you build a team focused on their role toward a unified vision.

Another let-go that spoke to me was Scott's view of the 5% solution. It's really difficult to solve 100% of the issues we face at any given time because we just don't know enough, don't have enough bandwidth to solve any particular problem 100% at any given point.

Scott challenges, "But what if you could just make it 5% better today? That doesn't sound like much. What if I did 5% every day? I'd be 25% better in a week. If I made it 5% better each week, I'd be 20% better in a month." In the interviews I've conducted of successful C-suite execs, what separates top performers is the ability to look at the issues the organization faces, then harness attention on the top three to four objectives that offer the greatest impact. Then keep moving the ball 5% at a time. Better beats best if you want fuel to drive things forward. What do you need to let go of so you can focus on what you can do better than yesterday?

Progress comes incrementally more than suddenly.

One day, you wake up and you've made major headway, where progress has now become a habit. It's taking those steps forward, incremental steps as opposed to quantum giant leaps.

So where's the line between micromanagement and accountability?

As the leader, what type of weather are you creating? Lightning bolts, thunderclaps, and howling wind create energy. But is it positive? Does it invigorate or scare, hampering creativity? Does it focus the team on compliance for survival or commitment to accomplish all that is possible?

By the way, we should be asking the same question when we walk into our homes.

Self-Reflection

Are you a thermometer (how effective do you measure the temperature in a room) or barometer (do you effectively monitor the pressure being felt)?

How well do you read nonverbal cues?

Describe a time that you were able to successfully change the atmosphere of a meeting.

CHAPTER 14

~~~

Are You Still Learning?

"Man's mind, once stretched by a new idea, never regains its original dimensions."

Oliver Wendell Holmes

I had the privilege of listening to Dr. T. Berry Brazelton, a world-renowned pediatrician, as he shared nuggets of wisdom on creating learning environments for youth from birth to adolescence. I sat in awe as this ninety-four-year-old young man poured out anecdotal strategies to engage infants, toddlers, and school age children.

His presence and ability to engage an audience that was thirty to fifty years younger than him was a testament that continued education and lifelong learning are the keys to adaptability in a changing workforce, maintaining a sharp mind, and longevity of purpose. During Dr. Brazelton's presentation his assistant who was about fifty years younger commented that Dr. Brazelton is a hard act to follow because of his "youthfulness" which he attributed to his insatiable desire to continue learning new things and teaching others. That's who I want to be!

Take the Challenge

Have you considered who and where you will be in the next ten, twenty, or thirty years? Will you continue to be a contributor in your chosen field of expertise, will you continue to be a trendsetter, a go-to person or will you become a liability, nuisance, and an artifact of the good ole days. Over the next month, take the challenge to develop and maintain a love for lifelong learning and professional development by pledging to two undertakings: commit to reading and take or teach a class.

According to the Associated Press in 2007 only one in four adults did not read a book that year.[8] Most individuals stop reading once they have achieved their high school diploma or degree. But the accomplishment of a diploma or degree is just the beginning. Continue reading books and articles in your chosen career. Benefits of reading include increased vocabulary and earning potential. The National Center for Education Statistics in 2003 reported that adults with low language literacy were three times more likely to live below the poverty level. Our children learn by example, so our commitment to reading becomes a legacy for them.

Our children learn by example, so our commitment to reading becomes a legacy for them.

Invest in yourself by taking classes or seminars throughout the year that enhance your career or business as well as enrichment classes that broaden your horizons. You also can challenge yourself by sharing your knowledge as an instructor; develop a curriculum or program and pitch it to your local association, ministry, or college. Teaching is a great vehicle to increase your knowledge and that of others.

Step outside your comfort zone and develop a relationship with someone outside your usual circle of associates and friends. This is an opportunity to educate yourself about other cultures, such as worshipping outside your faith occasionally or becoming involved in other organizations outside your culture. For example, I served for two years on the Asians Against Domestic Abuse board of directors. It was an excellent experience and insight into a culture and its people.

Take the challenge this month and expand your educational opportunities; and then make it a habit to adapt to the ever-changing workforce, nurture a sharp mind, and walk in purpose. Learning to learn is non-negotiable!

Deliberate Practice

You can become better at anything through deliberate practice.

Deliberate practice is the path to getting better results in any field. It's a specific method that makes the difference between an ordinary performance and an outstanding achievement. There are some guidelines for engaging in deliberate practice and specific applications for how to use it in your daily life.

The old adage that patience is a virtue couldn't be truer for deliberate practice. A large body of research confirms that it takes about ten years before most people develop into a virtuoso, whether you want to be a pianist or a titan of industry. Plus, that ten-year figure seems to be a minimum rather than an average.

As you would expect, you must practice regularly. Just like kids forget their course work during summer vacation, you may squander your efforts if you take prolonged breaks. Consistency is key.

Understand that there is a learning curve. It's natural to enjoy dramatic results when you first take up anything new. Then, you hit a plateau where you need to become more strategic if you want to keep advancing.

Identify the specific areas where you want to improve and focus your practice there. For example, you may have acquired an extensive vocabulary in French but need to spend time listening to native speakers to improve your pronunciation.

Be prepared for lots of repetition. The willingness to endure repetitive drills is what distinguishes the best performers. Keep in mind that the most productive methods may not feel like a lot of fun.

Keep your sessions relatively brief. Researchers have found that three to five hours a day is the absolute maximum for most people, spread over individual sessions of ninety minutes or less. Pace yourself according to the amount of time during which you can maintain an intense level of concentration.

Set specific goals. Use a blend of goals related to both outcomes and the process itself. The important thing is to approach your usual tasks with the mindset of becoming better at them.

Try to identify all the factors that go into your chosen experience. Keep adding to the list and experimenting with new combinations. For example, keep a journal so you can spot what conditions support or sabotage your healthy diet.

Outside observers may spot weaknesses that you fail to see. Partner up with a more experienced friend or hire a coach to get frequent feedback.

Evaluate your progress. Check in regularly to review how you're doing. Ask yourself what is going well and where you need to make changes.

There are many ways to specifically apply deliberate practice in your daily life.

You could enhance your exercise routine. Sports are one field where deliberate practice has been studied extensively. You can use the same techniques as professional athletes to get the most out of your yoga classes.

Music and other arts are also areas where practice obviously matters. So, get creative. You may want to resume the piano lessons you started as a child.

Perhaps you want to move ahead in your career. Any occupation can be broken down into tasks where you can make continual improvements. Brush up on your financial management skills or take a more systematic approach to making successful sales calls.

Deliberate practice principles can be employed to enrich your relationships too. Even interpersonal relationships have many aspects that respond to practice. Experiment with delivering constructive criticism more tactfully with your family and coworkers.

Deliberate practice requires time and hard work, but anyone can reap the benefits, regardless of whether you think you have any special innate talent for the activities you care about most. Focus on the areas where you want to improve and be patient. Over the long term, diligent repetition and targeted feedback will pay off.

Self-Reflection
What does learning mean to you?

What type of learner are you? Do you learn best by hearing, seeing, or hands-on (tactile)? If you have direct reports, do you know their learning preference?

When was the last time you initiated a learning goal for yourself and/or your team?

How was your commitment to learning affected during 2020 and why?

PART THREE

Mindset of
Relationship Management

Leadership is the art of providing opportunities for growth to those in your circle of influence. Extraordinary leaders are aware of the dynamics of relationship building. They exercise Emotional Intelligence muscles by being willing to actively listen, see others' points of view, and practice cultural humility.

Let's explore the power of being self-aware to holding yourself accountable, which opens the door to achieve extraordinary outcomes with what seems like ordinary people.

CHAPTER 15

~~~

Seeing Others' Perspectives

"Persons appear to us according to the light we throw upon them from our own minds."

Laura Ingalls Wilder

I can't stop thinking about her ... and my wife understands.

We had just returned from a trip to the Phoenician Resort in Scottsdale, Arizona, for a much-needed getaway weekend. For weeks we had run from one project to another at the office, the most recent a company party hosted at our house where we served 250 pounds of boiled crawfish (I'm a Cajun boy from south Louisiana) and entertained about fifty people. Needless to say we were totally spent and our weekend was most welcome.

We talked about Emily all weekend.

Emily Cortez

The facilities were impressive, the grounds immaculate, the food exceptional, but we talked about Emily all weekend.

Emily Cortez was charged with taking care of our room, not exactly what some would consider the most high-profile position at the hotel. When she came to our room the first morning, within minutes you could easily tell that her heart was in her work. It was very important to her that she had prepared the room properly for us, that our needs were fulfilled, and expectations exceeded. As my wife and I are both highly allergic to feathers and down, we always call ahead to request that any down pillows or comforters be removed from the room before we check in. Even though we have done this countless times, I have always been amazed that never (*not once*) had those accommodations been taken care of.

Emily was different. It was important to her that our request was taken care of, that we were cared for, not that we just have our room cleaned. She went to great length to explain to my wife how she was able to get the glass shower door to shine and sparkle, which is no easy task. There was even an offer to help us find the cleaning supplies she used, even to the extent of volunteering to stop off on the way to work and pick some up for us. The pride she took in how well she did her work was evident. We found ourselves looking for her as we walked in and out of our room, hoping for another opportunity to get infused with her vibrancy, her joy.

Infusion of Caring

The focus of what seemed to be Emily's every action and thought was to serve. By focusing on the needs of others, seeking ways to reach out and care for those who were placed in her path created a peaceful, loving atmosphere. What I noticed was I had a desire to connect with her, looking forward to the brief moments of our paths crossing. Her walk became a magnet, drawing Tommie and me toward her.

How many times do we get caught up in our daily frustrations, in the interruptions, griping about the sometime mundane tasks that must be done but give back minimal satisfaction? Do we lose sight of opportunities that are presented daily to infuse someone with a smile, a helpful hand, a moment of thanks or encouragement, the chance to express to someone that signal that they are important to us? Are we putting emotional energy into those we interact with throughout the day or are we taking energy from them?

> *Are we putting emotional energy into those we interact with throughout the day or are we taking energy from them?*

Was our time at the Phoenician special, memorable? Yes, for the beauty of the facility, the phenomenal food, and exceptional service. What I find amazing is that my favorite memory of our trip was a smiling face, a gentle heart. Emily made us feel special, that we were her favorite guests (as I am sure she does with all of the guests she cares for) by the small steps she takes each day, consistently, and with purpose.

Emily has become an important part of my memory … and my wife is glad.

Self-Reflection

How often do you create time to focus on the needs of your clients or direct reports?

What would be the response from a client or direct report if they were asked what is the most memorable moment they have experienced with you?

CHAPTER 16

~⁓~

Ignite Employee Engagement

"In the past a leader was a boss. Today's leaders must be partners with their people ... they no longer can lead solely based on positional power."

Ken Blanchard

On most Fridays, Tommie, my wife, and I grab dinner and a movie to wind down from the hectic pace of trying to run our own businesses balanced with church and civic obligations. She wanted to see *A Better Life*[9] for weeks but it kept sliding to the bottom of the selection list. I'm glad it finally made it to the top because not only was it highly entertaining, it was a movie that keeps playing in my mind.

The story was built around a father-son relationship in California. The dad worked for a landscaping business and was an illegal immigrant desperate for some way to earn citizenship. The son was a typical teenage boy, trying to find his way through school, a girlfriend, no longer playing soccer, and trying to stay away from the pull of gangs in his neighborhood. Facing hardships unimaginable by most of us, the father was diligent in his example of responsibility and living a life filled with hope. Slowly, his son recognized the truth in his father, and drew closer. His father showed with his actions that the pursuit of hope for a better tomorrow is the fuel necessary to blast our way through the difficult moments that life throws at us.

Create an Atmosphere of Hope

This storyline got me thinking: Our primary mission as a leader is devotion to create an atmosphere of hope. I've often stated that hope is not a strategy. However, without hope there is no strategy.

So what steps do we take to create an environment that permeates hope? By asking ourselves a series of questions, we can explore what sort of atmosphere we create for our teams and loved ones.

Responsible people sometimes need help in being held accountable. Are you focused on accountability or results? Do you focus on the process and lose sight of the results you are seeking? Looking for obstacles that slow down activity or blur the vision of our associates sends a signal that we understand the difficulty of their role and we help provide solutions, not just reports.

A client at one of the largest energy companies in the world recently shared that some people drop into his office for direction that only takes five minutes, yet they stay to visit for twenty minutes. He pointed out that they seem to have more fire and focus. Are you open for chat time? As I reflected on his message, it dawned on me that those individuals felt connected to the organization due to the personal interaction with their manager. It doesn't take happy hour and a pitcher of beer to build productive work relations.

How much time do you spend in tune ups instead of the big annual review? Hallway chats, simple interactions after meetings to offer feedback, guidance or affirmation lets your team know you care about them. These actions raise the anticipation of long-range growth potential.

Mike Richter, CPA, former Tax Partner of BDO, one of the largest accounting and consulting firms in the country, commented that he focused in the interview on looking for someone's dreams. I thought this idea was somewhat odd for a firm that hired a drove of accountants each year. If someone has no dreams, the energy they bring into work seems to wane very quickly; if it shows up at all. Do the individuals on your team know that you know what is important to them?

At times we operate at what seems to be close to the speed of light. It is easy to get caught up being focused on what isn't done instead of what is accomplished. Do you recognize the small steps taken daily or weekly? Newer people want to be involved and have an impact on the organization *today*! What they sometimes lack, however, is the business maturity to see the whole process or the steps required for successful initiatives. We don't have to be helicopter managers, yet we do need to help them see where they are in their growth cycle.

People want to perform, they want to be involved, and they want to contribute. As you walk around your office today, are you offering a path filled with hope or simply delegating tasks? I believe that hope is one of the magic keys that unlocks the doors of involvement, excitement, and performance standards well beyond what you might expect. How are you creating an environment that fosters productivity and engagement?

I believe that hope is one of the magic keys that unlocks the doors of involvement, excitement, and performance standards well beyond what you might expect.

Exercise: Am I Engaging My Team?

As a leader, you want your team members to be engaged and inspired in order to perform to their highest caliber. Explore the questions below for some self-discovery and to determine if you are such a leader.

Do I truly listen? You don't know everything. Your employees will often have excellent suggestions that can prove to be very beneficial. Listening is a valuable skill in many facets of life.

Am I perceived as fair? Few things breed resentment and discontent like unfairness. Treat all employees fairly and equally. When one employee is treated more favorably than the rest, you're headed for challenges.

Do I extend support and reassurance? Many people are too afraid or uncertain to do their best work. Part of your responsibility is to diminish those fears in your employees. Confident employees can accomplish more. Imagine how you'd perform if your boss wasn't supportive or reassuring. Now multiply that across several employees.

Am I a micro-manager? If you've hired the right people, you shouldn't need to manage every detail. Too much oversight instills a lack of confidence and robs your employees of enthusiasm. Have you ever had a boss who didn't trust you to handle anything autonomously? How did you feel about that boss?

How often do I show appreciation? Hard work is easier to swallow when people are thanked for their efforts. Words are free. Be generous with them. Employees love to feel appreciated for their work. Have you ever gone above and beyond in the workplace and had your efforts go unnoticed? How likely would you be willing to put forth the same effort again in the future?

Am I willing to take the blame? There are two kinds of bosses – those who shift the blame to an employee and those who absorb the blame themselves. Even as a child, you've been blamed for something you didn't do. How did you feel? Some things don't change in adulthood.

Do I schedule only necessary meetings? Few things are more soul-sucking than a meeting that accomplishes nothing. Keep meetings short, have an agenda, and take care of business efficiently.

Am I too busy to provide constructive feedback? Employees like to know when they're doing well. They also like to know when they're not. Let your employees know how they could be doing better.

Self-Reflection

Is my self-worth as a leader based on giving direction or support?

Is my mode of communication correction or connection?

How often do I ask for others' opinions before I give direction?

Is it easier for me to take credit for something rather than the blame?

CHAPTER 17

~⌒~⌒~

Does Praise Trip Your Trigger?

"Nothing else can quite substitute for a few well-chosen, well-timed, sincere words of praise. They're absolutely free and worth a fortune."

Sam Walton

I propped the mop against the wall, moved the couch back in place in my parents' home. News of my dad, Joe, battling lung cancer tilted my world off its axis. The only thing I could think of doing to help, since I had no medical training, was to clean the floor. To do … something … anything …

Before jumping into the car to head back home to Houston, I stood on his driveway trying to connect one more time. I started telling stories of my latest adventures, when suddenly I felt prompted to stop mid-sentence and shifted the focus to how important he had been in my life. As I intently watched his face to see if the words were having the impact I wanted, I noticed he had shifted his stance, crossing his arms across his chest. Gently, I reached forward to pull them down. "Dad, I really need for you to hear these words." As I continued speaking, tears welled up in his eyes, the corners of his mouth trembling.

Accepting Praise

Pop had a hard time accepting praise. How about you?

Emotional Intelligence requires that we process praise, and allow others to share observations on where we are having an impact. I'm not talking about the "aw shucks" kind of false humility moments as we shuffle our feet.

Accepting praise is different from seeking it. Our impact as leaders is not caused by being an approval seeking missile. Many times we have to make difficult decisions and deliver hard-to-hear messages. We offer a gift to others when we allow them to speak into us, to acknowledge their message has meaning to us.

Offering Praise

Do you find offering praise to be awkward, or fear it is perceived as false platitudes? "You mean I have to give them an attaboy for just doing their job?" High performing teams require that each member bring their own motivation, drive, and determination. Those are not traits we can instill in someone. The purpose of praise is not to make someone falsely feel good. Proper praise communicates to someone that they have value or importance. It signals that you notice their effort and contribution.

Proper praise communicates to someone that they have value or importance. It signals that you notice their effort and contribution.

Ken Blanchard points to this in his amazing book, *The One Minute Manager,*[10] which sold over 15 million copies and was published in forty-seven languages. (The latest release is an updated version, entitled the New One Minute Manager.) He highlights the importance of catching people doing things right, and praising them immediately. It creates an environment that motivates energy release, talent, and engagement.

It is the manager's job to keep in mind the importance of catching people doing things right and praising them immediately.

It remains one of the most powerful tools a leader can use to encourage and motivate people. Praise the person as soon as possible after you catch them doing something right. Let people know what they did—be specific.

Tell them how good you feel about it.

Then pause for a moment to allow them to feel good about what they've done. Encourage them to do more of the same, and make it clear you have confidence in them and support their success.[11]

While it is critical to stay focused on the mission and be in the "do" mode, we can't take emotion out of how we interact with those who are choosing to follow us.

There is nothing false about praise when delivered with the right purpose.

On that driveway, my dad's life continued to be used to teach me, shape me. There was such clarity in the importance of both receiving and offering praise and affirmation. As I drove off, I watched through the rearview mirror as Dad turned to walk toward the house. His shoulders more erect, the marine corps strides returning, steps more purposeful and powerful. I recognized how filled I was from pouring back into him, my words finding a home in his heart from making him feel cared for.

Self-Reflection
How often do you block what someone is trying to convey to you because of the emotional door that might be opened?   *Does offering praise make you feel uncomfortable or fake? Is your focus on intent or how you might look in delivering it?*   *Who do you need to "catch 'em doing something right?"*   *Is there anyone who you have not recently communicated their value to you? At work or home?*

CHAPTER 18

~~

Emotional Intelligence Coaching

"Peace is not the absence of conflict but the ability to cope with it."
Mahatma Gandhi

My daughter Nikki has been in sales since birth. At two years of age, she would stand in front of the fireplace holding court to all who would listen, valiantly trying to convince us of what seemed like some great observation in her life. Her challenge was that she had not yet learned to form words, only childlike babble. This did not slow down her passion or zeal. With arms flailing, she attempted to lead us on some journey, conforming us to her beliefs and viewpoints.

Learning from the Young

I watched her up-sell my friend, James Delmonte, Girl Scout cookies like a seasoned warrior when she was only ten. She called him on the phone as she had for five years, each year finding some way to increase the purchase amounts. Her last year, when he told her how many boxes to order, James (being the competitor he is) upped the amount to five boxes of each cookie selection. This amounted to thirty-five boxes of cookies.

Proudly, I listened in as I thought she was closing the order and asking for payment. Instead, she congratulated him by telling him he bought enough to be her *second*-best customer. After a pause, James apparently asked how many her top client bought. Calmly, with nerves of steel, she told of the 70-year-old Girl Scout (like the marines, no such thing as an ex-Girl Scout) who lived down the street from us who bought six boxes of each for her brother. I was beaming when I heard Nikki thank James for increasing his order to seven boxes each.

As she was winding up the sale and thanking him for again being her number-one customer, I nearly fell to the floor when she closed by saying, "Mr. Delmonte, I was looking at my form and it just dawned on me how easy it would be to turn sevens to look like nines." James had fallen into the trap of a true professional!

She has continued to be a great teacher in my life. Unfortunately, I, at times, have been a slow student.

Out at dinner one evening, Nikki began to present her request regarding an opportunity she had to travel on a school trip. After what I thought was an appropriate period of listening to her points, I began to implement parental discretion and governance on why it was not appropriate due to scheduling and cost. A sullen look fell over her face as the conversation came to a halt. In frustrating silence, I tried to understand why she shut down the interaction while we ate the rest of our dinner.

Back at home I asked my wife, Tommie, why teenagers had such a difficult time discussing things. As I expounded on how text messaging, instant message, twitter, and e-mail were destroying our youths' ability to communicate, she quietly pulled me aside, and pointed out that I was the one to build the dam preventing interaction. My response to Nikki left no room for her to feel understood. At no time did I confirm that I heard the request or expressed that I was open for her to discuss her wishes; I only point out why I felt it was not an option.

This was a painful learning experience that at times I still wrestle with. My role as father is to protect, provide, be the go-to guy who can solve matters, make things happen, just like the weight we sometimes place on ourselves as leaders.

These experiences, along with others, have helped me to develop my Triple A Process for coaching with an Emotional Intelligence schema. There are three steps to the process.

1. Ensure the person feels understood.

2. Ask clarifying questions.

3. Offer alternate solutions.

Ensure They Feel Understood

Before we move into resolution mode or guiding someone through views conflicting with ours, the first stage is to acknowledge that we have heard what was said. The message I sent to Nikki was that I didn't care about her view or outlook. This important, yet usually skipped, opportunity is essential in having the person we are talking to hear our viewpoints. Their mind will remain closed to our input until they feel understood. Notice I did not say "agreed with."

Their mind will remain closed to our input until they feel understood. Notice I did not say "agreed with."

So, the first step in the Triple A Process is to make sure the person we are interacting with feels understood. Only then will they lower their guard or defensiveness to outside information, alternate views, or suggested options. The axiom of Steven Covey's *The 7 Steps for Highly Successful People*[12] states that we must "seek first to understand before being understood." This concept is essential for creating an environment where someone feels valued and their input matters.

There is reason I stated that hearing someone is not the same as agreeing with them. I have to fight my hesitancy to go down this road. Allowing your teammate the grace of having their idea or request being heard will not be interpreted as accepting their point of reference or request. This step is simply capturing the message you heard and repeating it in your words, allowing them to confirm you understood their intent and offer any edits.

No acknowledgement, no affirmation means barriers will remain to any guidance, clarification, or explanation we might offer.

James was amazing in his support for the Girl Scouts and Nikki. However, I believe he was relieved when Nikki went to college.

Ask Clarifying Questions

Whoever restrains his words has knowledge, and he who has a cool spirit is a man of understanding. (Proverbs 17:27)

Notice how in the Road Runner cartoon, the Coyote never gave thought to gathering data? He consistently came up with some lame idea to solve the problem of capturing the Road Runner. Episode after episode he blew up, fell off a cliff, ran into a wall, shot himself in the foot. He thought that springing into action was the answer to his dilemma. What would he have accomplished with only a few additional questions of the Road Runner's intent or purpose for his next move? Fewer laughs but also fewer scars.

As leaders we are programmed to spring into action, remove the obstacle, or resolve the issue. Great leaders focus on making sure they have the necessary army flanking them to ensure success in taking the hill for which they are responsible.

Asking questions – especially ones that elucidate the conversation – is the second step of the Triple A Process. Emotional responses can thwart our ability to slide into questioning when someone's request or version of a story flies in the face of what we may deem logical, adult, or fair.

According to Dr. Rob Pennington of Resource International, an international expert on effective communication in the office and at home and author of *Find the Upside of the Down Times*,[13] questions are essential in providing a gateway for someone to feel understood and many times appreciated. After affirming what is being conveyed, asking questions sends a signal that you regard what is being said as important and allows for defining areas where assumptions or misinterpretations can be identified and corrected.

We are listening to clarify the intent of the person's message to us, so make certain you are listening without an agenda. Look out for two words running through your mind "Yes, but...." or possibly "but you don't understand." Maybe the trigger word here is "but." Have you ever found yourself in the middle of attempting to answer someone's question and you are sure of your answer but can't remember the question? Could be a signal of whose agenda you were focused on.

To clear up any discrepancies, look for words that may be vague or need acceptance of a common definition. This is again difficult because we hear words or phrases like "lots of," "all the time," or "as hard as I am working" and we begin a counterattack. The word "attack" here is appropriate because we will have to scale walls and cross moats charged with emotion. Granted some of the questions or suggestions may belong in Ripley's Believe It or Not collection. Sincerely asking for an understanding of the points they are making lowers the draw bridge, allowing you to better find common ground.

After repeating what you've heard, ask if there is anything additional you need to understand. This is an amazing question! What is added to the conversation is normally not something that is small in the other person's mind. Give great weight as you prepare your response to what they add and you will find your input will be much better received.

Their mind will remain closed to our input until they feel understood. Notice I did not say "agreed with."

The purpose of asking questions is to complete the process of making sure you are perceived as understanding all of the issues. This removes the words "yes but" or "but you don't understand" from forming defensive barriers in their mind.

And then you can do a most important step – agree with as much as you can!

Offer Alternate Solutions

The door is now open for the third Triple A Process's stage – alternate solutions. You've drained the emotional roadblocks that prevent dialog and increased the possibility of discussion rather than argument and defensiveness on either side. Now you can offer conflicting opinions, suggestions, or direction with a greater chance they will at least be heard, if not adhered to.

Next time these steps may keep you from falling off a cliff or blowing yourself up.

Self-Reflection

Have you worked with a coach?

Do you provide coaching to your direct reports or new team members?

Do you find yourself sometimes having difficulty listening during coaching or conversations with your direct reports or others during meetings? If so, what is the number one block to listening?

Brainstorm a strategy to remain open and actively listening during coaching sessions and meetings.

CHAPTER 19

~~~

Over Communicate by Shutting Our Mouths

"The most important thing in communication is to hear what isn't being said."

Peter F. Drucker

A t a time where companies are searching for leadership styles and processes to gain maximum performance, Shelly White serves as a new breed of leader. She is an amazing example of the shift from the "my way or the highway" mentality to "empowerment and engagement" that builds productivity and retention.

Shortly after receiving a degree in fashion merchandising, Shelly worked in a sales training program and then joined a company her father had started, the **Baro Companies** : http://barocompanies.com/, a manufacturer's representative and stocking distributor for complex engineering solutions. Her role was to help drive sales for an industrial equipment and supply company focused on serving the energy industry. Not an easy task for a twenty-something female entering a predominantly male-oriented industry. Yet within fourteen years, Baro grew from a $10 million company to over $60 million in sales.

After earning her stripes over ten years of rotating from the shop floor through business processes and into the inside and outside sales force, Shelly was asked to take over the role of president. The timing was critical as growth had stymied, calling for a change in a heavy-handed style of management.

Management – Not the Center of the Universe

Shelly had seen firsthand that fear or threats caused productivity to be sporadic, with no sustained energy. "No gun, no action takes place. Remove treats and productivity slides." Her attitude became "Management should not be the center of the universe. Let's see how far and wide you can share credit, let the people in the trenches win, not me. After all they are doing all the work."

We no longer have a business environment that allows leadership to expect people to follow us simply because of our title. Do we think they have to acquiesce or be grateful they have a job? There is a false sense of the impact unemployment figures have. Shelly and I laughed at the statistic both of us heard – within ten years, people will have seventeen jobs by the time they are thirty years old. This statistic was probably derived by the same person who declared that with the advent of computers we would all be working a thirty-two-hour work week, requiring the government in the 1980s to conduct research studies on what we would do to fill our time.

Post-pandemic national unemployment averages that hovered around 6% were very misleading. Statistics for white collar, highly skilled talent drastically dropped to between 2-3% or at times, even less. Shifting demographics pointed to even greater hiring and retention challenges in the near future. Baby boomers that had delayed retirement were leaving the workforce in staggering numbers.

Today, leaders must own the understanding that people choose the leaders they follow. Generational issues cause motivational and, at times, communication differences between the Baby Boomers, X and Y generations and the Millennials. Yet Shelly's experience has been that across generational lines, everyone is looking for a home, a place they feel inspired. Her experience is that there is a deeply held desire in all people to feel a part of something.

Listen to Employees

Baro's growth was anchored by the retention of key, highly productive staff. This was heavily influenced by Shelly's view that "the role of a leader is to listen to the employee, realizing most of the time the person reporting to us knows much more than we do about clients and field operations." By blending the information mix of what they know with what the leader knows, intellectual synergy is created, driving results and earning buy in from the team.

Their mind will remain closed to our input until they feel understood. Notice I did not say "agreed with."

This means the key to leadership success is empowerment through *over-communication.* During difficult times of falling sales, major clients shifting vendors, and unexpected service delivery issues, leaders earn their roles by the way they communicate with all staff. Shelly's mantra is, "Be honest, be specific, and be genuine. Give the real facts. And something that is difficult for most leaders, let them talk."

During one stage of Baro's growth, Shelly assumed the role of overseeing the production shop. Rather than trying to prove how much she knew to earn allegiance, she walked into daily meetings asking for the shop team to help her out, because one of their clients had a major problem they needed to fix. She laid out what needed to be accomplished and asked a simple question "Who is going to make sure that happens?" After a few seconds, a hand from the back of the room raised and a voice said, "I'll take it on."

A hard part of Shelly's journey has been to take a back seat. "I've had to learn to let my team run with the responsibility to get the required result. You'll be surprised at how often they'll come up with great solutions especially if they felt heard." State the problem, allowing someone to take ownership. Evaluate the obstacles or difficulties that might arise, be a resource or advocate ensuring the person is successful. This is empowerment.

How often, as leaders, do we spend time trying to figure out what to say in order to handle a situation, rather than considering what questions we should be asking and what opinions we should be seeking? An award-winning, long-tenured senior sales person shared with me recently that the reason she has stayed with her current company was, "I feel listened to; I get to offer my opinion." I was shocked when she shared that 75% of the time her ideas were not implemented. Her reply was simple, "But at least I get a voice." *I get a voice.*

Shelly's message challenges all in leadership today. *How do we give those who choose to follow us more of a voice?*

Self-Reflection

Think of a time when you wanted to contribute to the team and felt silenced by either the manager or other more seasoned team members.

Describe the feelings that silenced you.

Describe a time that you may have inadvertently silenced a direct report or team member.

How often do you ask for feedback or create time for brainstorm meetings?

CHAPTER 20

Are You Throwing Shade?

"Show me a successful individual and I'll show you someone who had real positive influencers in their life."

Denzel Washington

"Throwing shade" is a pop culture term that means to make a condescending or sarcastic comment, making someone feel inferior.

Let's change the narrative of "throwing shade" to encompass an exemplary practice of creating opportunity and space for others to be cultivated so that they can sustain until they are able to independently grow on their own. During my career I have had mentors and supervisors in my life who threw shade on me as I grew into a leader.

This is known as the skill of social responsibility; the desire and ability to willingly contribute to society, your social group, and generally the welfare of others. Many large organizations actually have a social responsibility department.

During the pandemic of 2020 there was the opportunity for leaders of organizations on a global level to pivot and make contributions to the team members through flexible schedule, remote officing, donating to non-profit programs, and mentoring aspiring leaders within their organizations. Leadership is envisioning the future while recognizing inequity, barriers, and opportunities to be innovative, even if you will not be the beneficiary of the outcome.

> *Leadership is envisioning the future while recognizing inequity, barriers, and opportunities to be innovative, even if you will not be the beneficiary of the outcome.*

Social Responsibility

Let's delve into some ideas to grow Emotional Intelligence by integrating social responsibility into your leadership regiment on a daily basis.

Seek out an employee who is different from you (i.e., race, gender, political affiliation, age, etc.) and offer to mentor them on the unwritten rules of the organization and/or the majority group. Even if this individual takes the information gleaned and moves on to another position, organization, or starts their own company, you have played a role in their success and modeled for them the importance of being inclusive and seeking out talent.

There are times that you and the team you are working with may come to an impasse on an issue. Be willing to see another person's point of view. Often times our gut response is to dig in because we believe in our own point of view. However, if championing another vantage point does not go against your moral or ethical code, is it possible that by coming to agreement with an alternate point of view you may provide opportunities that are good for the overall organization. For example, perhaps you are no longer of childbearing age and the company is deciding about creating a policy and procedure that provides parental leave after a family has a new baby so they do not have to use their regular leave. Championing this does not directly provide support for you, however, the company overall may be able to retain top talent with that policy.

Give colleagues and team members their flowers while they can enjoy them. Kouzes and Posner, leadership experts, share that "encouraging the heart" is one of the exemplary practices of the world's most effective leaders. The simple gesture of saying thank you, great job, or spotlight people for doing good work goes a long way.

Self-Reflection

How often do I ask questions before expressing my thoughts or beliefs to better understand someone's experience or perspective?

Do I use sarcasm in place of humor to gain attention or even express affection?

On a scale of 0 to 5, where do you land as a mentor? Zero is no mentoring skills and five is the best. Describe the reasoning for your rating and what is one step you can take in the next twenty-four hours to move the needle on your rating by one point.

Do you have mentees (formal or informal) that are different from you in either race/ethnicity, gender, age, socio-economics, etc.? If yes, what have you learned from them in the process of mentoring them? If no, make a decision to set a date for reaching out to someone different than yourself and approach to be a mentor within the next three months.

Describe a time that a mentor or supervisor created an environment that made you feel insecure or unwelcome. How can that experience help you to be a more extraordinary mentor/supervisor?

CHAPTER 21

～✦～

How to Handle Difficult Conversations with Grace

"You're not learning anything unless you're having the difficult conversations."

Gwyneth Paltrow

Effective communication is the cornerstone of great relationships. Whether you're communicating with friends, family, coworkers, your partner, or even strangers, everything goes smoother with effective communication. You get more of what you want and the other party is happier too.

Even difficult conversations – when handled with grace and composure – can be beneficial to your relationships.

Skills for Improving Thorny Talks

Consider using these tips the next time you face a tough conversation.

1. *Face the issue as soon as possible.* It's tempting to put off difficult conversations. However, not dealing with the issues can make them worse. In addition, it can prolong the anger and

resentment you feel. Find the courage to face the other person and make the conversation happen.

2. *Prepare before the conversation.* Consider all aspects of your concerns. You may benefit from making a list of points you need to discuss. How will you address these issues? Try to find the heart of the issues, so you don't get lost during the conversation. A good analysis can save you time and effort later.

3. *Decide what you want to accomplish.* What is your ultimate goal with this conversation? It's important to have clear goals in mind ahead of time so you can stay on topic.

   o   What kind of an outcome do you want?

   o   Do you want to see things change? In what way?

   o   Do you want the other person to apologize?

4. *Give yourself time to calm down before you discuss the issue.* If you're angry or hurt, it may not be the best time to talk. It's more effective to enter a difficult conversation with a calm attitude. If you're too hurt to see past the emotion, put off the conversation until later. Try to see the issues from multiple perspectives and the other side.

5. *Understand the importance of silence.* Silence isn't a bad thing during a difficult conversation. You don't have to fill every minute with words. Silence can be used to give you both a break and a chance to figure out what to say next. It can help you analyze the previous words. Pauses can also help you both maintain calm.

6. *Watch your emotions.* During the conversation, you'll benefit from controlling your emotions. Focus on staying positive and calm. Exerting discipline to your feelings may not be easy, but it's important. Difficult conversations can dissolve into madness if emotions take over. Try focusing on the other person's feelings and long-term impact of your behavior.

7. *Think about your relationship.* Friends, coworkers, spouses, family members, and others have unique relationships with you. The way you talk to them will stay in their memory.

> ***Difficult conversations are easy to ignore, but ignoring them is a slippery slope into frustration.***

Difficult conversations are easy to ignore, but ignoring them is a slippery slope into frustration. Instead of hiding from the issues, consider how you can resolve them. Your relationships will benefit greatly when you can work together to find solutions.

Learn to handle these tough conversations with grace and, over time, you'll find fewer and fewer issues that you have to resolve.

Self-Reflection
Is there a conversation that I've been delaying (okay, avoiding) that I need to address? *What do I do that may create barriers when I attempt to have difficult conversations (do I avoid, talk too much, talk over someone)?*

CHAPTER 22

~⌣~

Are You Looking Up High Enough?

"Like, with one arm I know I can surf, but competitive surfing can be really frustrating, and sometimes you don't do as well as you want to. It can be discouraging at times. But whenever I do get frustrated, I just focus on God."

Bethany Hamilton

In Chapter 12 I referenced how fear had been crippling my life with overwhelming panic attacks. When I was in my early twenties, I moved to Houston, Texas, from Louisiana. My job was to be a corporate recruiter, a headhunter. I joined a firm growing at the speed of a rocket ship and hit the fast track. We opened forty offices in two-and-a-half years.

On a recruiting trip to San Francisco, I fell asleep on the plane, exhausted from the frantic pace we had been keeping. Suddenly I woke, but not from turbulence. My palms were sweating, my heart pounding, and I felt like I was going to come out of my skin. The only thought in my mind was, "I have got to get off this airplane!" Luckily, and don't ask me why, I remembered that airplanes were not made to let people off at 34,000 feet.

The next week, back at home, I visited a client on the fiftieth floor of One Houston Center. As the elevator climbed, I looked down to see sweat dripping out of my hand like a faucet. You know how they say that 60% of your body is water? I truly thought I was leaking. As the elevator doors finally opened, I stepped out, only to see the floor rolling up and down.

After a series of medical tests, I was diagnosed with a condition referred to as "agoraphobia." Agoraphobia is a disorder in which you experience repeated attacks of immense fear and anxiety, also referred to as "panic attacks." Dreading the overwhelming physical sensations that arise without warning, and at times for no recognizable reasons, causes a fear of places where escape might be difficult.

So, massive panic attacks became a part of my daily life. They would happen whenever I climbed on an elevator, rode an escalator, stood in line at a grocery store to buy a candy bar. If I was driving my car in the right-hand lane and tried to move to the left-hand lane, I couldn't do it. I would have to move back into the right-hand lane. It was impossible to drive across a bridge or overpass. My world started closing in, becoming smaller and smaller.

Through medicine and counseling, the symptoms began to subside, but my anxiety continued to manifest itself.

Fast forward to when my daughter Nikki (at 14 years of age) and I were in the mountains of California for a father-daughter vacation at the JH Ranch. These vacations became our tradition after her mom and I got divorced. As we checked-in upon arrival, the people at the front desk started explaining what our week was going to be like.

I was told that I would spend the next week exploring the forest on cables 35 feet up in the air on high rope courses. My agoraphobia began to rear its ugly head and I looked at her and practically shouted, "You and what army?" But my daughter looked so excited, I couldn't let a little life-threatening anxiety attack ruin a perfectly good bonding opportunity.

After a week of surviving aerial crossing cables, there was the last event of the week, the last thing we had to do before I was paroled. It was called "The 757." It was a 50-foot-tall telephone pole with a 14-inch-by-14-inch platform attached to the top. Our job was to climb the pole, swing up onto the platform, and then jump off and catch a trapeze that was inconveniently located 7 feet above my head and 7 feet in front of me, hence 757. Once I caught the trapeze, a college kid, with not nearly enough training I thought, would use the rope system to lower me down to the ground, most likely kicking and screaming – me, not him.

Standing at the foot of this death pole, I was certain that somebody was trying to kill me. Thinking of jumping off a perfectly good, albeit tiny, pole made my heart thunder in my chest and my chest tighten in fear. But my daughter was there and she didn't have the years of built-up anxiety that I did. In fact, when she saw the pole, what do you think she said? "That looks so fun, Dad." At that moment I really began to believe she had been adopted.

Because of my battle with anxiety attacks, it was always important to me that I not build fear in my daughter. So our motto was simply that "It is okay to be afraid, but it's not okay to not try." We stood there looking at that pole together and she turned, saying, "I think I will go first." Mustering every ounce of fatherly guidance and direction I replied, "That's a great idea."

She walked to the pole of death, grabbed the rungs, and began her climb. The next thing I knew she stood on top of the platform, jumped off and just barely missed the trapeze. She swung from the rope securely holding her and yelled down that she wanted to try again.

It took her three tries to capture that trapeze but she was finally able to make it. I looked into her brave eyes, I took her cheeks in my hands, and said, "Sweetheart, Dad enjoyed watching you so much. Want to take my turn?"

Nikki smiled at me with a sparkle in her eye. "I want to see you do this Daddy!"

I walked over to Marty, the young college guy who was sitting there holding the protective rope. And I explained to him, "I am having some pretty bad back spasms right now." He said, "Sir, you are the last one for the day. Let's shut this thing down and you can just go home."

With great trepidation I retorted, "I have to at least try. I will try to make it halfway up the pole, and then if I can't go any further, I will just jump off." Marty replied, "Not a problem."

Walking about 25 feet back, I turned and looked at the pole. I don't know what you believe, but I know that I have a Creator and He has made me, with wonderful things in mind of what He intends for me, if only I look in the right direction.

Every time I grabbed the rung, and for the first time in my life, I simply said, "I can do all things in Your name. I can do all things in

Your name. I can do all things in Your name." Halfway up the pole my back spasms were gone.

"I can do all things in Your name. I can do all things in Your name. I can do all things in Your name."

I continued climbing up the ladder until my fingers were on top of the platform. All week long the dads had all been together, encouraging and challenging each other – Dwayne from Alabama, Darby from California, Charlie from Florida. All of us had been tethered with a special bond that came from the love we shared for our daughters. Clinging to the top of the pole, I could see my team crowded together on the ground, all shouting and cheering me on. But out of all of that noise, there was one little voice that stood out. It simply said, "You can do it, Daddy. You can do it."

The next thing you know, I'm standing on top of a 14-inch plate with only one thought in mind, "Who, in their right mind would jump off of a perfectly good pole?" Screaming at the top of my lungs, I jumped and captured the trapeze.

Bending the Mirror

That day my life changed. I recognized the things that stop us from moving forward are the times we lose focus on a higher power and allow handcuffs of fear, doubt, worry, anger, anxiety to be created. We use the desire to control our circumstances and situations to accomplish, to battle, to achieve. Yet, when we shift focus to our Creator, turning away from focusing on ourselves to lean into Him, we are blessed with amazing fruit – Love, Joy, Peace, Patience, Kindness, Goodness, Faithfulness, Gentleness, Self-Control.

Notice how the fruit falls in line with the Emotional Intelligence we've been referencing. In order for me to be released from the bondage I was experiencing, I literally had to look up and let go. When I did, I received two blessings. First, my panic attacks disappeared to never return. And second, a thirst to spend time reading in order to try to understand what it meant to seek His will in my life.

Fear, concern, worry is what makes us look into a mirror at ourselves and then turn it into a funny mirror like you see at a carnival. You know the one that bends everything? But when we look to God as we face the situations or circumstances we battle, the mirror straightens. It becomes the key that unlocks the door to who we truly are, releasing us to turn steps into leaps toward who we are intended to be. The door swings wide open for us, releasing the most amazing dreams that you could possibly have and transforming them into reality.

I now know that when I look up, I'm a better boss, co-worker, friend, husband, and father. It's a vision we pray you enjoy as well.

Self-Reflection

What are you hesitant to believe, do, or say that is holding you back from being what God intends you to be?

Is there a belief about yourself or your ability that fear is using to "bend the mirror" when you look at yourself, warping your perspective of the possibilities God has for the relationships in your life?

CHAPTER 23

Final Prompts

"Owning our story and loving ourselves through that process is the bravest thing we'll ever do."

Brené Brown

Ten Secrets to Grow as an Emotionally Intelligent Leader

1. *Brag!* Keep a journal or notebook with you throughout the day. Write down your accomplishments as they happen. Many people believe they will remember them later. You won't, especially on a "not so great day" or during a stressful season at work. Don't leave it to chance; record your victories in your "Brag Book." When you need a reminder of what you are bringing to the table, open your book and have a personal brag session.

2. *Get a little help from your friends.* Use your social media connections to build your brand. Reach out to your network of "friends" who have worked with you at a job or in community organizations. Ask them to give you one word that

describes your contribution to the team. Their feedback will provide insight into how those closest to you value your efforts.

3. *Talk back … to yourself.* Stress can make you turn on yourself. It is common that people in high-stress positions become over-critical of themselves because of their need to control amidst chaos. When you find yourself questioning your abilities, disengaging from work, or having self-defeating thoughts, stop immediately. Combat negative thoughts with constructive words. Say out loud, "It's okay. I'm okay. I've got this." Mantras such as these cause you to be more mindful of the thoughts you are incubating. Only select words that build you up and increase your confidence.

4. *Count yourself out.* It's simple and it works. Before you launch into a series of thoughts or actions that deflate your ego (or could end your career), simply count backwards from ten. Breathe between each number. This will halt negative thoughts and give you time to think of different alternatives instead of reacting to each situation. In fact, try it now. Inhale, hold it for at least ten seconds, and slowly exhale. Yeah, that's it!

5. *Walk this way.* When you are at odds with a coworker or superior, pause and put yourself in their shoes. Imagine what it feels like to see life from their perspective. You know how you feel, but have you stopped to consider how they feel? You can't ask others to be empathetic toward your point of view without also doing the same for them. They may have rubbed you the wrong way through their method of communicating

their thoughts, but there may be elements of truth in what they're saying nevertheless.

6. *Clone yourself.* Replace yourself via mentoring, coaching. Create opportunities for those who are eager to take on additional responsibilities. They will appreciate the experience and visibility; you will appreciate the extra help. Having another set of hands to assist you will relieve some of your stress and will free up time that you can use to focus on bigger projects.

7. *Get some face time.* Approximately 85% of people are met with conflict in the workplace. Unresolved conflicts can drain your inner drive. Schedule the time to meet face-to-face with people with whom you have a conflict and deal with it directly. Don't rely on written communication to resolve your issue. It won't work. Use this opportunity to grow relationships, embrace diverse views, and regain harmony within your work family.

8. *Celebrate Yourself.* You are always there cheering on others and celebrating their accomplishments. Take the time to celebrate your accomplishments. So often women who are driven tend to have a checklist and simply mark off their accomplishments. Try actually taking the time to celebrate yourself by taking a day off, buying something you have been wanting or simply taking a few minutes to close your eyes and embrace yourself in a hug and say "good job!"

9. *Tell the truth.* We are living in a time that people are craving the truth, however, expecting a "lie." Be willing to tell the truth to yourself about you, and also be willing to tell the truth to

those who are following you. This simply means holding people accountable, challenging them in love to tell the truth about themselves and, most importantly, tell the truth about the things that need to be addressed.

10. *Embrace diversity.* Our world is changing by the second and those who will be successful are the ones who are willing to leverage diversity. Take the time to research and actually hold conversations with those who are different from you. Yes, this means you may experience discomfort, and that is where the growth occurs and the *bold*ness emerges!

From Our Hearts to Yours

Dear Leader,

The opportunity to build, nurture, and promote greatness in yourself and others is an amazing gift and responsibility. It is leadership, and leadership is not about the title that you wear; it is about a mindset.

The mindset of leadership is challenged by our history, beliefs, attitude, feelings, and determines our behavior as a leader. What does all this have in common? It is the ability to create, learn, and *unlearn* patterns on how we respond to life. It is learning to understand why we believe what we believe and how those beliefs impact our feelings and ultimately how we behave in our personal and professional relationships.

It is our hope that the messages shared throughout *EQuip to Lead* are opportunities for you to choose to pivot on your leadership journey so that you can experience an extraordinary mindset that transforms how you see yourself and the lives of those you touch.

You are not ordinary. The fact that you chose to read this book signifies that you are striving for more than a title or corner office; you desire to embrace true happiness and to contribute to the world through collaboration that showcases the diverse talent that comes together to build businesses, organizations, and families that celebrate humanity.

Thecia & Mike

ENDNOTES

Human Versus Business – We Need Both Sides
[1] Jeff D. Reeter, *Do Life Differently: A Strategic Path Toward Extraordinary* (New York: Hatchette Book Group, 2020).
[1] https://www.inc.com/jessica-stillman/eq-matters-more-than-iq-for-group-success-new-harvard-study-says.html
[1] Jill Hickman Companies Authorized Partner network offers services that include leadership development training, executive coaching, and corporate university curriculum development. See: https://jillhickman.com.

Chapter 1: To Tell the Truth
[1] James M. Kouzes and Barry Z. Posner, *The Leadership Challenge: How to Make Extraordinary Things Happen in Organizations* 6th ed. (New Jersey: John Wiley & Sons, Inc., 2017).

Chapter 4: Embracing Feedback … Perception Is Reality
[1] James C. Hunter, *The Servant: A Simple Story About the True Essence of Leadership* (New York: Crown Publishing Group, 2012).

Chapter 10: Understanding and Managing Your Emotional Triggers
[1] Travis Bradberry and Jean Greaves, *Emotional Intelligence 2.0* (San Diego: TalentSmart, 2009).

Chapter 13: Leaders Control the Weather!
[1] Scott Eblin, *The Next Level: What Insiders Know About Executive Success,* 3rd ed. (Boston: Nicholas Brealey Publishing, 2018).

Chapter 14: Are You Still Learning?
[1] See: http://spinuzzi.blogspot.com/2007/08/one-in-four-adults-read-no-books-last.html?m=0

Chapter 16: Ignite Employee Engagement
[1] Chris Weitz, *A Better Life* (US: Lime Orchard Productions, 2011).

Chapter 17: Does Praise Trip Your Trigger?
[1] Ken Blanchard, *The One Minute Manager* (New York: Berkley Publishing Group, 1985).
[1] Ken Blanchard and Spencer Johnson, *The New One Minute Manager* (New York: HarpersCollins Publishers, 2015).

Chapter 18: Emotional Intelligence Coaching
[1] Steven Covey, *The 7 Steps for Highly Successful People: Powerful Lessons in Personal Change* (New York: Simon & Schuster, Inc., 1989).
[1] Dr. Rob Pennington, *Find the Upside of the Down Times: How to Turn Your Worst Experiences into Your Best Opportunities* (Houston: Resource International, 2011).

Appendix A

Emotional Intelligence Worksheet

Emotional Intelligence affects your relationship in so many ways! Use this worksheet to build your self-management skills. Your teammates at work and home will be pleasantly surprised by the difference!

Self-Awareness

How well do you understand yourself?

What are some of your triggers for positive emotions, such as happiness? How do you communicate these to others at work or home?

What are some of your triggers for negative emotions, such as sadness or anger? How do you communicate these to others at work or home?

Identify one of your relationship mistakes. What can you do to correct this mistake?

List three of your most important values. Do you live these values? Give an example of a time when you demonstrated these values.

Exercise: The Seven Day Challenge

For the next week, review each day and consider your answers to these questions.

- How did you spend your time?

- What did you enjoy?

- What did you dislike?

- Did you lose your temper or experience depression? If so, why?

- What was the best thing that happened to you? What was so great about it?

- What was the worst thing that happened?

- What would you change about the day?

- What did you learn about yourself today?

- How did you do in your relationships today? What did you learn about your teammate(s)? What could you have done better?

Self-Management

Practice self-soothing: What are some positive ways that you can count on to uplift your mood? What are some more ways that you would like to try?

Practice self-discipline: What are three things that you know you should do but have been putting off? Do them and congratulate yourself for your self-discipline!

Think of a decision that you've been struggling with to make. Look at the situation from a long-term perspective. Looking at it this way, what are your best options? Pick one and run with it.

- Describe an instance in which you had trouble controlling your emotions and demonstrated poor emotional self-regulation. What were the results?

- Describe an instance in which you were able to control your emotions and demonstrated strong emotional self-regulation. What were the results?

- Make a plan for how you can respond positively and effectively when your negative emotions are triggered.

Relationship Management

When was the last time that you focused on your coworker (or family member) and really listened to what they had to say – without judging, assuming anything, or interrupting? How can you build more of this into your daily routines?

Do you struggle to be able to see things from another's perspective? How can you practice this skill?

Social Skills

Practice asking open-ended questions

- What are some open-ended questions that you can ask someone that you've just met at a social gathering?

- What are some open-ended questions that you can ask someone at work or home?

List three sincere compliments that you can give someone today and then do it. Plan to give a sincere compliment at least once each day. (If this feels like a stretch, it sounds like it is a muscle that needs to be strengthened.)

What are some sincere compliments that you could give to your coworkers?

What are some sincere compliments that you could give to a stranger that you encounter in your daily routine, such as someone waiting in the same line as you?

Do you know what your body language says about you? What? How can you make some changes so that it will show others more of what you'd like to communicate?

Appendix B

Six Skills that Will Increase Your Emotional Intelligence

Emotional Intelligence is considered a much better predictor of success than pure intelligence. In many cases, it doesn't matter how intelligent you are.

You know plenty of people that possess average intelligence that are very successful. The struggling genius is quite common. There's more to life than being able to do calculus in your head.

Making good decisions, communicating effectively, having positive relationships, and managing yourself well can be far more valuable and powerful than a genius-level IQ.

Boost your Emotional Intelligence with these strategies.

1. *Become an excellent listener.* Think about the best listener you know. You probably hold that person in high regard. Listening is a lost art that few people are interested in resurrecting. During your next conversation, notice what happens while you're speaking. The other person is likely bored, distracted, and simply waiting to speak.

You'll do much better with people and have fewer misunderstandings if you put all of your attention on the other person during a conversation. They'll even think that you're a great conversationalist. Try it and see!

2. *Pause before you respond.* Think of all the times you wish you'd kept silent. Taking a moment to collect your thoughts can be a real advantage. You'll save yourself a lot of grief if you give yourself the opportunity to respond wisely, or to not respond at all. Give yourself all the time you need to make an intelligent decision.

3. *Develop self-awareness.* Very few people are self-aware. We have little idea of how others perceive us or how we come across to them. Think about how odd it is to hear a recording of your own voice, or how you seem to look heavier in photos than you thought you were. That's only the beginning!

You might be significantly more rude or obnoxious than you think. Maybe you're dismissive to others and don't even know it. Ask someone you trust what they think your biggest problem is. You may be surprised by what you hear. You won't like the answer, but you'll know in your heart that it's true.

4. *Learn how to motivate yourself.* Life is easy if you can get yourself to do the things you know you should do. However, few of us are effective in motivating ourselves to do those things consistently. You can avoid most of the drama life has to offer if you can simply do the things that need to be done, when they need to be done.

Consider why you procrastinate when faced with tasks that are unappealing to you. You're going to have to do them eventually. Why not put yourself out of your misery as soon as possible and simply get them done?

5. *Analyze your emotions.* Notice your emotions while you're experiencing them. Try doing this in place of quickly responding to them.

For example, if someone says something that irritates you, rather than reply in a hostile manner, ask yourself why you're experiencing this emotion. What caused it? Is it reasonable? What is an intelligent way to respond?

6. *Be assertive.* There are advantages to being assertive. You have a much better chance of getting what you want. You'll also be more transparent to others. People won't have to guess what you want from them. If you are upfront with your feelings and concerns, your relationships will have fewer misunderstandings, too.

Emotional Intelligence might be what you're missing from your life. You can be goal-oriented, committed, and capable, but it's difficult to rise above the level of your Emotional Intelligence.

How would you rate your Emotional Intelligence? In what areas could you improve?

Appendix C

The Everything DiSC Agile EQ Learning Experience

Everything DiSC® Agile EQ™ is a virtual or classroom training and personalized learning experience that teaches participants to read the emotional and interpersonal needs of a situation and respond accordingly. By combining the personalized insights of DiSC® with active Emotional Intelligence development, participants discover an agile approach to workplace interactions and learn to navigate outside their comfort zone, empowering them to meet the demands of any situation. In this training, participants will discover their EQ strengths, recognize their EQ potential, and commit to customized strategies for building agility. The result is an emotionally intelligent workforce that can support your thriving agile culture – no matter where they are.

The Everything DiSC Agile EQ Profile provides participants with valuable insights that allow them to discover an agile approach to workplace interactions. In this personalized, 26-page profile, participants will discover their DiSC style, learn about the instinctive mindsets that shape their responses and interactions, recognize opportunities to stretch beyond what comes naturally to them, and gain actionable strategies to become more agile in their approach to social and emotional situations.

Mike Lejeune & Thecia Jenkins

For more information contact

Mike Lejeune   Thecia Jenkins

mike@mikelejeune.com   thecia@theciajenkins.com

AUTHORIZED PARTNER

JHC JILL HICKMAN —COMPANIES—

THE AUTHORS

Mike Lejeune

Based in Houston, Mike has a passion for developing tomorrow's leaders. One of the first independent consultants to join the Jill Hickman Companies Authorized Partner Network, Mike is a keynote speaker, master workshop and retreat facilitator crafting programs designed to enhance leadership effectiveness, Emotional Intelligence, culture shaping, and communications. With more than twenty-five years in leading companies and industry trade associations, Mike built Lighting the Path Consulting to help ignite the fire in people to stretch their horizons and realize their importance in the lives that surround them. He served as president of Steverson & Company, one of the top executive search firms in Texas.

He has presented workshops across the US, Canada, and South Africa. Each keynote, workshop, and consulting project Mike leads focuses on reasons that today's workforce becomes disenfranchised and offers techniques and strategies industry champions use to lead high performing organizations. His programs address the how-to for building sound engagement techniques and, more importantly, challenges the "why" behind approaches and strategies to offer new windows into current-day business solutions.

Mike is the host of the podcast series *Strategies for Tomorrow's Leaders*, where he discusses leadership principles with nationally renowned experts. He is the author of the highly regarded blog,

Lighting the Path, and, along with his daughter Nikki, is the co-author of the award-winning book, *A Father's Love: The Generational Bridge that Changes Hearts Forever.*

Thecia Jenkins

Thecia has been using the power of relationship to deliver transformational training to law enforcement, healthcare providers, educators, victim service providers, and corporate teams for twenty-five years. Her areas of expertise are intimate partner violence, Emotional Intelligence, and interpersonal communication. Thecia has certifications in DiSC, Emotional Intelligence, Diversity, and Mediation.

She has trained and provided consultation on intimate partner violence and Emotional Intelligence to audiences in West Africa (Ghana), Trinidad & Tobago, and London. Thecia was also featured on the Oprah Winfrey Network reality show, *The Book of John Gray,* as an expert on sexual violence.

Thecia is an independent consultant and also works with the Harris County Domestic Violence Coordinating Council as the Training Director where she develops and delivers programs for first responders to survivors of domestic violence and also provides technical assistance to public sector professionals and human resource managers.

She is passionate about equipping organizations to maximize the value of their teams.